Unemployment Experience

of Individuals

Over a Decade

Variations by Sex, Race and Age

D0020960

PY- AST- 83

Herbert S. Parnes

Rutgers University
Institute of Management and Labor Relations

and

Ohio State University
Center for Human Resource Research

This monograph was prepared under a contract with the Employment and Training Administration, U.S. Department of Labor, under the authority of the Comprehensive Employment and Training Act. Researchers undertaking such projects are encouraged to express their own judgments. Interpretations or viewpoints contained in this document do not necessarily reflect the official position or policy of the Department of Labor.

The W. E. Upjohn Institute for Employment Research

Library of Congress Cataloging in Publication Data
Parnes, Herbert S., 1919-
  Unemployment experience of individuals over a decade.

  1.Unemployed—United States—Longitudinal studies.
I. Title.
HD5724.P352   1982   331.13'7973   82-15948
ISBN 0-88099-002-3 (pbk.)

iii

167641

The Author

Herbert S. Parnes is professor of Industrial Relations and Human Resources in the Institute of Management and Labor Relations at Rutgers University and a part-time senior research associate in the Center for Human Resource Research at The Ohio State University, where he is also Emeritus Professor of Economics. Between 1965 and 1979 he directed the National Longitudinal Surveys of Labor Market Experience at Ohio State under contract with the U.S. Department of Labor. During that period he and his associates produced 19 volumes of reports on the NLS data, of which the most recent was *Work and Retirement: A Longitudinal Study of Men* (MIT Press, 1981). Parnes continues to do research based on the National Longitudinal Surveys, of which this monograph is an example.

Acknowledgments

This report was prepared under a contract with the Employment and Training Administration, U.S. Department of Labor, under authority of the Comprehensive Employment and Training Act. Researchers undertaking such projects under government sponsorship are encouraged to express their own judgments. Interpretations or viewpoints contained in this document do not necessarily represent the official position or policy of the Department of Labor or of the W. E. Upjohn Institute for Employment Research.

The author expresses his indebtedness to Howard Rosen for suggesting the topic, to Lawrence Less for his very capable research assistance, to the data processing staff of The Ohio State University Center for Human Resource Research for serving as intermediaries with the computer, to Gilbert Nestel for valuable consultation on the preparation of the paper, and to Michael E. Borus and Steven Hills for their useful comments on an earlier draft. None of these individuals, of course, is implicated in whatever inadequacies exist in this final product.

Executive Summary

Taking advantage of data from the National Longitudinal Surveys of Labor Market Experience, this report analyzes the unemployment experience during a recent decade of four subsets of the U.S. labor force: men who at the end of the decade were 26-34 and 55-69 and women who were 26-34 and 40-54 years of age. Although the data for each group span a ten-year period, information on unemployment is available for only eight of the years, and thus understates both the incidence and amount of unemployment over a full decade.

Large proportions of individuals with labor force exposure experience some unemployment over a ten-year period: majorities of young men and women and three or four out of ten of the older groups. The unemployment that occurs is very unevenly distributed within each of the cohorts. The 10 percent of the unemployed who had the longest cumulative durations accounted for between 35 and 40 percent of all the unemployment that occurred during the decade under review. When those with no unemployment are also considered, the 5 percent of all individuals with the most unemployment accounted for over one-half of all unemployment among the older men and between 29 and 45 percent in the other three cohorts.

Unemployment means not only the lost earnings attributable directly to the periods of enforced idleness, but leads also to long term reductions in earning capacity, especially among the younger men and women. For example, the 1976 earnings of young men with chronic unemployment (at least 66 weeks during the period) were $1.43 lower than the earnings of comparable men with no unemployment, and the corresponding wage penalty for the chronically unemployed young women was even higher.

Multivariate analysis reveals that the characteristics that bear the strongest and most consistent relationship with the incidence and/or duration of unemployment are educational attainment, occupational and industrial affiliation, interfirm mobility, and length of service in the job held at the beginning of the decade. Nevertheless, these factors, together with several others that are found to be related to the incidence or duration of unemployment in one or more of the cohorts, account for only small proportions—in the range of 10 to 25 percent—of the total variation in unemployment experience. A substantial amount of unemployment experience appears to result either from being in the wrong place at the wrong time, or from personality characteristics that generally go unmeasured. This conclusion is reinforced by an examination of selected case studies of the chronically unemployed. There is clearly no singular explanation for the phenomenon.

The findings have both discouraging and encouraging aspects. From an egalitarian perspective, the extreme concentration of the economic and psychological burdens of unemployment among relatively small proportions of labor market participants is cause for concern, especially in view of the evidence that unemployment produces a long term deterioration in earning capacity. On the brighter side, the fact that the temporal distribution of chronic unemployment is similar to that of total unemployment and that both are responsive to variations in general economic conditions tends to dispel the most pessimistic interpretations of structural unemployment. On the theoretical level, the findings make suspect the modern neoclassical interpretations based on search theory, according to which all unemployment is really voluntary.

Contents

Introduction 1

From official Current Population Survey data on labor force and employment status and annual work experience, it has long been possible to infer that (1) the longer the reference period, the greater the incidence of unemployment; and (2) irrespective of the length of the reference period, the distribution of unemployment is far from random.[1] The first of these phenomena is attributable to turnover among the unemployed; the latter to the fact that a variety of economic, demographic, and perhaps personality characteristics are correlated with the likelihood of becoming or remaining unemployed. However, until the emergence of longitudinal data sets during the past decade, it has not been possible to generate reliable estimates of the number of individuals who experience varying amounts of unemployment over periods longer than a year. The National Longitudinal Surveys of Labor Market Behavior (NLS) and the Michigan Panel Survey of Income Dynamics (PSID) have provided opportunities to investigate questions of this kind. Using these data sets, the incidence and/or the determinants of unemployment over periods longer than a year have been studied by Kohen (1971), Dickinson (1974), Gramlich (1974), Feldstein (1975), Clark and Summers (1979), Corcoran and Hill (1979), and Parnes and Nestel (1980).

This paper is a modification and substantial expansion of the 1980 study. It analyzes the unemployment experience over the major portion of a decade of each of four NLS cohorts: young men (1966-1976) and young women (1968-1978) who were 26 to 34 years of age at the end of the relevant decade, women (1967-1977) who were 40 to 54 years old at the end of the period, and older men (1966-1976) who had attained 55 to 69 years of age by the terminal year. It is the first longitudinal study that examines the long-run unemployment experience of women as well as men.[2] For the four groups under consideration, four major questions are addressed: (1) What was the distribution of the samples, by race, according to the cumulative number of weeks of unemployment? (2) What are the correlates of having experienced some unemployment during the decade? (3) Among individuals who suffered some unemployment, what characteristics are associated with its cumulative duration? (4) Controlling for other factors, what effect did cumulative unemployment during the decade have on the earning capacity of the respondents by the end of the period?

In the remainder of this section, the character of the data is described in somewhat greater detail. Section II describes the extent and distribution of unemployment among the four cohorts, and Section III analyzes the correlates of both the incidence and duration of unemployment. Section IV compares the hourly earnings records of individuals without unemployment and those who experienced moderate and substantial amounts of joblessness. Section V provides additional insights into the anatomy of chronic unemployment by a brief examination of selected cases. The final section summarizes the findings and offers concluding observations.

The Data Base

Although data for each of the four cohorts extend over a 10-year period, we have information on unemployment for a total of only 8 years. In each case these represent the 12-month periods immediately preceding the surveys (or the approximately 24-month period between the 1969 and 1971 surveys in the case of the two older cohorts).[3] For individuals who were not interviewed in one or more years but who had returned to the sample by the final year, imputations were made by attributing to each such year the average number of weeks of unemployment experienced in the remaining years, although the average figure was arbitrarily increased by four weeks when the reason for noninterview in a particular year was inability to locate the respondent, on the assumption that unemployment was more likely in such cases. Special rules were also used for periods following military service for which data were incomplete. The decision rules for these imputations are available from the author.

The universe of males covered by the analysis are those who were interviewed in 1976 and who had spent at least one week in the civilian labor force (or in the armed forces in the case of the young men) *in each* of the 12-month periods covered by the data. However, young men were excluded if they were enrolled in school at the time of the initial survey (1966). Since the imposition of these criteria would have made the size of the women's samples too small for meaningful multivariate analysis, the universe of each cohort of women was defined to include those who spent at least one week in the civilian labor force *at any time* during the period covered by the data. Sensitivity analysis has shown that measures of the incidence and the distribution of unemployment are remarkably insensitive to these variations in the specification of the universe (see appendix tables A-1 and A-2).[4]

Nevertheless, in interpreting the data, it is important to keep several points in mind. First, because they cover only eight years, the data obviously understate both the incidence and duration of unemployment over the full decade. Second, the restriction of the universe of young men to those who were not enrolled in school in 1966 means that the 1976 sample overrepresents high school dropouts and underrepresents college graduates. This means that the data tend to overstate the incidence and the annual average duration of unemployment during the preceding decade among the total group of men who were 26 to 34 years of age in 1976. However, the exclusion from the NLS sample of young men who were in the armed services in 1966 but later rejoined the civilian population operates in the opposite direction. The exclusion of individuals who dropped out of the sample and were not interviewed in 1976 is a source of downward bias in all of the estimates of total unemployment over the decade, since we have evidence that the individuals who dropped from the sample had a somewhat higher incidence and somewhat higher average duration of unemployment prior to their departure than did individuals who remained in. Finally, intercohort comparisons of the incidence and distribution of unemployment are affected by the fact that there is a slight variation among the several cohorts in the specific years of the decade that are covered, during which there was variation in the national unemployment rate.

Extent and Distribution of Unemployment   2

Incidence

The proportion of individuals who experienced some unemployment over the 8-year period varied substantially among the several cohorts (table 1). It was as low as 29 percent among the older males[5] and as high as 68 percent among the younger group of women. Occupying intermediate positions were the older group of women (40 percent) and the younger group of men (53 percent). Within each cohort there were perceptible racial differentials in favor of the whites, but these were much more pronounced among the younger than the older men and women. In both of the younger groups, whites were twice as likely as blacks to escape unemployment over the period—a percentage point spread of 23 in the case of the males and of 17 among the females. In contrast, among the older cohorts the black-white differential was slightly under 10 percentage points.

For purposes of this paper, the "chronically unemployed" are defined as those who cumulated at least 66 weeks (one and one-fourth years) of unemployment over the relevant time period. When attention is focused on this group, the differences among the several cohorts are not so pronounced, the proportion ranging from 3 percent of both

Table 1
Percent Distribution of NLS Cohorts by Cumulative Duration of Unemployment Over Preceding Decade, 1976-1978[a]

Number of weeks	Males[b]						Females[c]					
	Age 26-34			Age 55-69			Age 26-34			Age 40-54		
	Total	White	Black	Total	White	Black	Total	White	Black	Total	White	Black
None	47	50	27	71	72	63	32	34	17	60	61	52
1-9	23	23	22	10	10	13	31	32	25	17	18	15
10-25	15	14	20	6	6	10	18	18	20	10	9	15
26-65	11	10	18	8	8	9	16	14	28	9	9	13
66 or more	5	3	12	4	4	6	3	2	9	3	3	5
Total	100	100	100	100	100	100	100	100	100	100	100	100
Mean	13	11	26	9	9	12	13	12	25	9	9	14
N	1275	945	330	2248	1652	596	3031	2211	820	3343	2377	966

a. Percentages may not add to 100 because of rounding. Data cover only eight years of the decade ending in 1976 for the males and in 1977 and 1978 for the older and younger women, respectively. For a more detailed description of the data, see text.

b. Excluded from the data are men not interviewed in 1976, those who were not in the labor force (or armed services, in the case of the younger men) at least one week in *each of the years* covered by the surveys, and those young men who were enrolled in school in 1966.

c. Excluded from the data are women not interviewed in 1977 (older women) or 1978 (younger women) and those who were not in the labor force for at least one week during *any of the years* covered by the surveys.

groups of women to 4 and 5 percent of the older and younger men, respectively. Despite the greater incidence of unemployment among the young women, the average cumulative duration was identical for the two young groups—13 weeks; for both the older men and women the average was 9 weeks.

Distribution of Unemployment
by Duration

When attention is confined to those individuals who experienced some unemployment during the decade (table 2), the older men had the most unfavorable record; mean duration was 31 weeks, and 14 percent of the group met the criterion of chronic unemployment. Next were the young men and the older group of women, with very similar distributions around a mean of 24 weeks in each case. Somewhat over two-fifths of each group were unemployed for less than 10 weeks; exactly 9 percent of each were chronically unemployed, with durations of 66 weeks or longer. Here the similarity ends, however, for the young men were far more likely than the older women to have had repeated spells of unemployment. Three-fifths of the women but less than two-fifths of the young men had all their unemployment confined to a single year; only 6 percent of the women but a fifth of the young men were unemployed in four or more years. On the basis of this criterion the young men's record was also worse than that of the older men, among whom 16 percent were unemployed in as many as four years.

Despite the fact that the younger group of women had the greatest incidence of unemployment over the decade, their unemployment was of shorter duration than that of any of the other three groups—on average, four weeks below that of the young men and older women and 11 weeks below that of the older men. Chronic unemployment was also con-

Table 2
Selected Data on Distribution of Unemployment Over the Decade Ending in 1976[a]: Members of NLS Cohorts Who Experienced Some Unemployment

Measure	Men 26-34[b]					
	Total		Whites		Blacks	
	Percent of persons	Percent of unemployment	Percent of persons	Percent of unemployment	Percent of persons	Percent of unemployment
Cumulative number of weeks of unemployment						
Less than 10	43	8	46	10	31	4
10-25	28	19	28	22	28	13
26-65	20	37	19	39	25	31
66 or more	9	36	7	30	17	51
Total	100	100	100	100	100	100
Mean number of weeks	24		21		35	
Number of years in which unemployment occurred						
1	37	11	39	13	29	6
2	26	19	26	20	25	19
3	19	20	18	21	20	16
4	8	16	7	15	12	19
5 or more	11	34	10	32	14	40
Total	100	100	100	100	100	100

Table 2 (continued)

	Men 55-69[b]					
	Total		Whites		Blacks	
Measure	Percent of persons	Percent of unemployment	Percent of persons	Percent of unemployment	Percent of persons	Percent of unemployment
Cumulative number of weeks of unemployment						
Less than 10	36	5	36	5	35	5
10-25	22	11	22	11	26	14
26-65	28	37	28	37	24	33
66 or more	14	47	14	47	15	47
Total	100	100	100	100	100	100
Mean number of weeks	31		31		32	
Number of years in which unemployment occurred						
1	46	16	47	16	39	16
2	24	24	24	24	25	18
3	14	19	14	19	16	18
4	6	11	5	11	11	18
5 or more	10	30	10	30	10	30
Total	100	100	100	100	100	100

Table 2 (continued)

Measure	Women 26-34[c]					
	Total		Whites		Blacks	
	Percent of persons	Percent of unemployment	Percent of persons	Percent of unemployment	Percent of persons	Percent of unemployment
Cumulative number of weeks of unemployment						
Less than 10	45	9	48	11	30	4
10-25	27	22	27	24	25	13
26-65	23	48	22	48	34	47
66 or more	5	21	3	16	11	36
Total	100	100	100	100	100	100
Mean number of weeks	20		18		31	
Number of years in which unemployment occurred						
1	39	15	41	17	27	8
2	27	24	27	25	29	21
3	17	23	17	24	19	20
4	11	22	10	21	14	23
5 or more	6	16	5	13	11	28
Total	100	100	100	100	100	100

Table 2 (continued)

Measure	Total		Women 40-54[c] Whites		Blacks	
	Percent of persons	Percent of unemployment	Percent of persons	Percent of unemployment	Percent of persons	Percent of unemployment
Cumulative number of weeks of unemployment						
Less than 10	44	7	46	8	31	5
10-25	24	17	23	16	31	18
26-65	24	41	23	41	28	42
66 or more	9	35	8	35	10	35
Total	100	100	100	100	100	100
Mean number of weeks	24		23		28	
Number of years in which unemployment occurred						
1	60	30	61	30	52	26
2	22	28	22	29	25	24
3	12	24	11	23	16	31
4	4	11	4	10	6	14
5 or more	2	7	2	8	1	5
Total	100	100	100	100	100	100

a. See footnote a, table 1.
b. See footnote b, table 1.
c. See footnote c, table 1.

siderably less prevalent among them than among the other three groups.

The pattern of racial differences that characterizes the incidence of unemployment prevails also with respect to duration. By whatever measure one chooses to examine, blacks fared less well than whites; by most measures the differences were more pronounced in the younger than in the older cohorts. For example, among the total samples of young men and young women, mean duration of unemployment was 13 to 14 weeks longer for blacks than whites, while for the two older groups the racial difference was only 1 to 5 weeks.

Relative measures of unemployment. The comparisons up to this point have been in terms of the absolute amount of unemployment experienced by the several cohorts. Another perspective that may be of even greater interest—particularly in comparing the male and female cohorts—is the proportion of their labor force weeks that were spent on layoff or looking for work. This ratio, expressed as a percentage, is conceptually equivalent to an unemployment rate for each individual.[6] Tables 3 and 4 show the distributions of these rates for each of the cohorts, by race.

Comparison of the data in tables 3 and 4 with the absolute distributions in table 2 reveals at least two interesting differences. First, because of the differences in labor force exposure between men and women, use of the unemployment ratios causes the record of joblessness for the women to become less favorable relative to the men than when absolute measures are used. The mean ratio[7] for the older group of women is highest, at 9.4 percent, compared with 8.2 percent for the younger women, 7.9 percent for the older males and 5.9 percent for the younger males.

This may be looked at from another point of view. In a relative sense, the unemployment ratio of 15 percent or more

Table 3
Ratio of Weeks of Unemployment to Weeks in the Labor Force
Over Preceding Decade, 1976[a]: Men with Some Unemployment[b]

Ratio: weeks unemployed x 100 weeks in labor force	Age 26-34			Age 55-69		
	Total	White	Black	Total	White	Black
Less than 2.5 percent	46	49	33	37	37	35
2.5-4.9 percent	17	17	17	15	15	16
5.0-9.9 percent	17	17	18	20	20	19
10.0-14.9 percent	9	8	12	11	11	11
15.0-19.9 percent	5	4	10	7	6	8
20.0-24.9 percent	3	3	2	4	5	3
25.0-29.9 percent	1	-	3	2	2	2
30.0 percent and over	2	2	6	3	3	6
Total	100	100	100	100	100	100
Mean ratio[c]	5.9	5.3	8.8	7.9	7.9	8.3
N	726	484	242	687	465	222

a. See footnote a, table 1.

b. See footnote b, table 1.

c. Σ weeks unemployed $\div \Sigma$ weeks in labor force.

Table 4
Ratio of Weeks of Unemployment to Weeks in the Labor Force
Over Preceding Decade, 1976[a]: Women with Some Unemployment[b]

Ratio: weeks unemployed x 100 weeks in labor force	Age 26-34			Age 40-54		
	Total	White	Black	Total	White	Black
Less than 2.5 percent	31	33	20	30	32	23
2.5-4.9 percent	15	16	11	16	16	15
5.0-9.9 percent	19	19	19	16	15	21
10.0-14.9 percent	11	11	12	10	10	9
15.0-19.9 percent	8	7	11	6	5	7
20.0-24.9 percent	3	3	4	3	3	4
25.0-29.9 percent	4	3	5	4	4	4
30.0 percent and over	9	8	17	15	14	17
Total	100	100	100	100	100	100
Mean ratio[c]	8.2	7.4	12.6	9.4	9.2	10.5
N	2148	1465	683	1491	922	479

a. See footnote a, table 1.

b. See footnote c, table 1.

c. Σ weeks unemployed $\div \Sigma$ weeks in labor force.

may be regarded as equivalent to what we have defined as chronic unemployment, since for those continuously in the labor force for the full eight years, 66 weeks of unemployment is approximately 15 percent of the total number of weeks (8 x 52 = 416;   66 ÷ 416 = .159). Whereas chronic unemployment in the absolute sense was far more common among the men than the women in both the younger and older age groups, both groups of women were considerably more likely than the men to have cumulative unemployment ratios in excess of 15 percent.

Second, the position of the two groups of women relative to one another differs somewhat depending upon whether the absolute number of weeks of unemployment or the unemployment ratio is used as the criterion. The less favorable position of the older group of women is much less pronounced when labor force exposure is taken into account than when absolute measures of unemployment are used.

Concentration of Unemployment

In all four cohorts, and for blacks and whites alike, a substantial amount of the unemployment over the decade was concentrated among relatively small proportions of individuals (tables 5 and 6). The most fascinating aspect of the data is the similarity across the eight sex-age-race groups in the distribution of total unemployment among those who experienced any. The 10 percent of the unemployed with the most unemployment accounted for between 36 and 39 percent of all of the weeks of unemployment during the decade. When the effects of incidence and duration are considered jointly, the uneven burden of unemployment is, of course, even more pronounced, although there is greater variation among the cohorts and between blacks and whites. At one extreme stand the older group of men, among whom 5 percent of the sample accounted for over one-half of all the unemployment. The degree of concentration was almost as

Table 5
Selected Measures of Concentration of Unemployment: Men

Measure	Age 26-34			Age 55-69		
	Total	White	Black	Total	White	Black
Proportion of total unemployment attributable to:						
Top 10 percent of all respondents with unemployment[a]	39	38	37	38	39	36
Top 5 percent of all respondents[b]	37	38	34	53	54	44
Chronically unemployed[c]	36	30	51	47	47	47
Minimum number of weeks of unemployment for:						
Top 10 percent of all respondents with unemployment[a]	63	58	79	79	79	78
Top 5 percent of all respondents[b]	64	58	92	59	58	70

a. The 10th percentile, starting with respondent with the most unemployment (and excluding those with no unemployment).

b. The 5th percentile, starting with respondent with the most unemployment (and including those with no unemployment).

c. Respondents with 66 or more weeks of unemployment.

Table 6
Selected Measures of Concentration of Unemployment: Women

Measure	Age 26-34			Age 40-59		
	Total	White	Black	Total	White	Black
Proportion of total unemployment attributable to:						
Top 10 percent of all respondents with unemployment[a]	36	36	33	39	39	35
Top 5 percent of all respondents[b]	29	29	25	45	47	36
Chronically unemployed[c]	21	17	36	35	35	35
Minimum number of weeks of unemployment for:						
Top 10 percent of all respondents with unemployment[a]	51	46	70	62	61	66
Top 5 percent of all respondents[b]	58	52	84	55	52	65

a. The 10th percentile, starting with respondent with the most unemployment (and excluding those with no unemployment).
b. The 5th percentile, starting with respondent with the most unemployment (and including those with no unemployment).
c. Respondents with 66 or more weeks of unemployment.

great for the older group of women, of whom 5 percent accumulated 45 percent of the total amount of unemployment. Among the younger men and women, the corresponding proportions of unemployment were 37 and 29 percent respectively.[8]

Racial differences in the concentration of unemployment vary among the several cohorts when the effects of incidence and duration are considered jointly. In the two younger cohorts, because much larger proportions of blacks than of whites experienced chronic unemployment, the proportion of total unemployment attributable to the chronically unemployed was considerably larger among blacks than among whites; in the two older cohorts the differences were negligible. When the criterion is the amount of unemployment attributable to the "top" 5 percent of *all* respondents, the proportion is lower among blacks than whites in all four cohorts. Thus, considering the total population (and not merely those who experience some unemployment) the burden of joblessness, while heavier among blacks than among whites, is more equally distributed. In all cohorts, of course, the cumulative number of weeks unemployed of the fifth percentile is higher for blacks than for whites, e.g., 92 versus 58 weeks in the case of the young men.

While the foregoing variations are worthy of attention, the more important point is that the total amount of unemployment during the decade was distributed very unequally among those who were potentially exposed to it, and that this was true for both sexes and races and for the several age groups represented by the NLS cohorts. These extreme individual differences in the incidence and duration of unemployment invite attention to the sources of variation in unemployment experience, the subject of the following section.

The Correlates of Unemployment

3

The factors that are associated with the incidence of unemployment and its duration are explored by means of a multivariate analysis of three measures of unemployment experience: (1) whether any unemployment occurred, and, for those who experienced any, the cumulative duration expressed in terms of (2) total number of weeks and (3) as a percentage of the total number of weeks of labor force exposure. Appendix tables A-3 to A-6 present the results of multiple classification analyses for the four age-sex cohorts.[9] Each of these ascertains the net relationship of the several measures of unemployment experience to race, age, marital status, education and training, health condition, class of worker and industry, tenure in the job held when first interviewed, interfirm mobility over the decade,[10] and two social psychological variables—a measure of work commitment[11] and a measure of powerlessness (perceived locus of control).[12] Finally, the number of years in which the individual was not continuously iin the labor force is used to represent continuity of labor market experience.[13]

From this list of independent variables it should be clear that no formal model of the determinants of unemployment is being proposed. Some of the variables—e.g., years of schooling—may indeed be causal,[14] but others—e.g., mobility—are probably simply the concomitants of unemployment. The purpose is the modest one of uncovering the personal and economic characteristics of the members of the sample that appear to bear an independent relationship to either the incidence or duration of unemployment.

In the summary of the findings for each of the cohorts that is presented below there are instances in which variables having significant F-ratios in the MCA results are described as not being associated with unemployment. In virtually all of these cases the reason is that the significant F-ratio reflects the value of the "not ascertained" category, which is not shown in the table. Generally speaking, I have avoided generalizing about the significance of a variable unless the t-values for one or more categories (not shown in the tables) are statistically significant.

Men 26 to 34

The MCA results for the younger cohort of males are shown in appendix table A-3. The independent variables account for about one-fourth of the variance in the incidence of unemployment among young men and about 15 or 16 percent of the variance in the absolute and relative duration of unemployment among those who experienced some joblessness during the decade. With respect to both incidence and duration, there is a very substantial difference between black and white youth. The unadjusted data show a 23 percentage point differential between the incidence of unemployment of blacks and whites (73 versus 50 percent). Controlling for all other variables in the analysis reduces this by better than one-half, but still leaves a significant differential of 11 percentage points. Similarly, the adjusted differentials in the two measures of average duration are highly significant, with the values for blacks being half again as high as those for whites.

The substantial gross relationship between age and the incidence of unemployment disappears entirely when other variables—principally educational attainment—are controlled. Years of schooling bears the expected relationship with all three dependent variables. Neither training nor health, on the other hand, shows a comparable systematic relationship.[15] Marital status is strongly related to the unemployment experience of the young men; those who were married in both 1966 and 1976 had a lower incidence and a shorter duration than other young men. Occupation, class of worker, and industry are all significantly related to both incidence and duration of unemployment. Blue-collar workers fare substantially less well than white-collar workers. Government workers have a much lower incidence rate than private wage and salary workers; among the latter, construction workers have a greater incidence and a much larger average duration than other workers.

Young men who resided continuously in labor market areas with relatively low unemployment rates experienced a lower-than-average incidence of unemployment, but there was no comparable difference in duration. As would be expected, mobility status during the decade displays a very strong relationship to the unemployment experience of the young men. The adjusted incidence rate was only 33 percent for those who were with the same employer during the decade as compared with 58 percent for those who changed employers. Differences in duration between the two groups were equally impressive. Tenure in 1966 job is also a highly significant predictor of both the likelihood of subsequent unemployment and of its duration when it occurs.

Neither of the two psychological variables achieves statistical significance, although the small differences between "internals" and "externals" and between men with strong and weak work ethics are generally in the expected directions. Number of years with some time out of the labor force shows a strong positive relationship with the incidence of unemployment, reflecting the almost inevitability of unemployment among persons who move into and out of the labor market. With other factors controlled, service in the armed forces did not significantly increase the likelihood of some unemployment during the decade, but was associated with a longer cumulative duration for those who experienced any. Other things equal, veterans experienced an average of four more weeks of unemployment over the decade than nonveterans.

Men 55 to 69

The MCA results for the older cohort of males (appendix table A-4) show some similarities to, but also some marked differences from, the results for the younger men summarized above. Perhaps the most important difference between the two age groups is that for the older group, when other factors are controlled, there is no racial difference in unemployment experience. The 9 percentage point gross difference between blacks and whites in the incidence of unemployment is reduced to a nonsignificant net difference of 1 point, and there is no significant difference in duration, whether measured in absolute or relative terms. Neither health nor training is significantly related to the incidence or duration of unemployment. As in the case of the younger men, unemployment experience is related to marital status. Men who were married both at the beginning and the end of the decade had a lower incidence of unemployment as well as a lower average duration when measured relative to labor force exposure.

By all odds the strongest relationship with unemployment experience during the decade is manifested by the mobility variable. Among nonretired men, the incidence of unemployment, other things equal, was only about one-third as high for those who were with the same employer continuously through the decade as for those who were not. Duration of unemployment for those who experienced it was also much lower for the nonmobile men. Retired men, almost all of whom would by definition have changed employer, had a somewhat lower incidence of unemployment but a somewhat longer duration than the job changers.

Length of service in 1966 job was strongly related to the likelihood of experiencing some unemployment over the ensuing decade, but, unlike the case of younger men, not to its duration once it occurred. Adjusted incidence rates ranged from 41 percent of those with less than one year of service in their 1966 jobs to 24 percent of those with 20 or more years of service. Occupation, class of worker, and industry display substantially the same pattern for the older as for the younger group of men, although the industry differences are somewhat more pronounced for the former while the occupational differences are less pronounced, occurring in the incidence of unemployment but not in its duration.

Unlike the results for the younger cohort, the two psychological variables help to explain some of the variation in unemployment experience of the older group of men. Those who manifest a strong work ethic have a lower incidence and a shorter duration of unemployment than less strongly committed men. "Internal" men are less likely to become unemployed than their "external" counterparts; and while differences between the two groups in duration of unemployment are in the same direction, they do not achieve statistical significance. This finding is perplexing, for the variable had been viewed as a proxy for initiative and was therefore expected to be related to duration of unemployment as a reflection of less intensive and less imaginative job search by the externals (cf. Andrisani and Nestel, 1975).

Finally, number of years with some nonparticipation in the labor force bears a strong positive relationship to the incidence of unemployment, as it does for the younger group of men. In this case, however, it shows a weak inverse association with cumulative number of weeks of unemployment. The positive relationship with incidence reflects the unemployment that accompanies movement into and out of the labor market. The inverse relationship with cumulative duration probably reflects the fact that individuals cannot be counted among the unemployed while they are out of the labor force. In this connection, it should be noted that the relationship disappears when duration of unemployment is expressed as a percentage of weeks in the labor force.

Women 26 to 34 (appendix table A-5)

As was true for the young males, the racial differences in unemployment experience for the younger cohort of women are pronounced. Even controlling for other factors, young black women were considerably more likely than whites to have experienced unemployment (79 versus 66 percent) and of those who did, blacks averaged 10 more weeks of joblessness than whites. When weeks of unemployment are expressed as a ratio to weeks in the labor force, the percentage is almost four points higher for blacks than for whites.

Age also makes a difference among the young women, unlike the case of their male counterparts. Those who were 16 to 19 at the beginning of the decade were more likely than those 20 to 24 to experience some unemployment; however, duration was shorter for the younger than the older group, both when measured in absolute and in relative terms. Young women whose marriages were dissolved during the decade had a higher incidence of unemployment than those who were married both in 1968 and 1978 and those who became married during the decade, although the differences are not large. The longest duration figures are for women not married in either year, but this is at least in part a reflection of their more consistent labor force participation, for the differences are less pronounced when duration is measured in relative terms.

The existence of health problems among the young women has a consistently adverse effect on unemployment experience. Women who acknowledged health problems affecting work in either 1968 or 1978 (or both) had a significantly higher incidence of unemployment during the decade. For those experiencing unemployment, weeks unemployed as a percentage of weeks in the labor force was also significantly greater for those with health problems.

As in the case of the young men, educational attainment bears a strong inverse relationship with all three measures of unemployment experience. Moreover, for any given level of education as of 1978, those who had taken additional years of schooling during the decade had a higher incidence and longer duration of unemployment than those who had completed their schooling by 1968. On the other hand, there is no consistent relationship between training outside of regular school and unemployment experience.

Whether the criterion is the incidence or the duration of unemployment, blue-collar workers had less favorable experiences than white-collar workers. With regard to industrial pattern, women in government and finance were least likely to have experienced joblessness, but differences in duration of unemployment did not follow the same pattern. Moreover, the highly significant differences that exist in absolute number of weeks of unemployment become nonsignificant when duration is related to number of weeks in the labor force, suggesting that the differences reflect variations in labor market exposure.

Length of service in 1968 job is inversely related to the incidence of unemployment, but not to its duration. Mobility status bears the same strong relationship to the incidence of unemployment that has been observed in the male cohorts. Also comparable to the finding for young men is the fact that the incidence (but not the duration) of unemployment is significantly lower for women who resided continuously in local areas with low initial year unemployment rates. The number of years of less than full labor market participation bears a strong positive relationship with the incidence of unemployment and with the ratio of weeks unemployed to weeks in the labor force, but not to duration of unemployment measured in absolute terms.

Women 40 to 54 (appendix table A-6)

Among the older cohort of women the racial differential in the incidence of unemployment remains highly significant when other factors are controlled, although the difference is less pronounced than for the younger age cohort. The adjusted percentages are 46 for blacks and 39 for whites. There is also a barely significant racial difference in the duration of unemployment, but this becomes nonsignificant when duration is measured in relation to labor force participation, reflecting the greater participation of black women.

Curiously, age is inversely related to the incidence of unemployment, but not to its duration. There are rather pronounced differences in the incidence of unemployment, depending upon marital and family status. Women who were married at the beginning but not at the end of the decade were substantially more likely to have experienced unemployment than those who were married at both dates. Within marital status categories, the presence or absence of children under age 16 appears not to have had a consistent influence. The variation in total number of weeks of unemployment among the eight marital-family status categories is statistically significant, but defies generalization. In any case, the differences become nonsignificant when measured relative to number of weeks in the labor force, suggesting that they reflect primarily differences in labor force exposure.

There is a statistically significant relationship between educational attainment and unemployment experience, but with some unexpected irregularities. The adjusted incidence rate declines with increasing education, except for those with some college (but no degree), among whom the rate is higher than that of high school graduates. In the case of relative duration (expressed as a percentage of weeks in the labor force) those with college degrees have higher rates than any other educational category.

The acquisition of training outside the regular school system is unrelated to the incidence of unemployment but bears a highly significant relationship to cumulative duration when expressed as a ratio to total time in the labor force. Those with some training during the decade under consideration fared best, with the lowest adjusted rate being registered by those who had no such training prior to 1967 (12.8 percent). The worst experience was registered by women who had no training either prior to or subsequent to 1967, among whom the ratio was 17.4 percent.

Among women who were in the same local labor market area in 1967 and 1977, both the incidence of unemployment and the cumulative duration were slightly lower in areas with low unemployment rates in 1967. As might be expected, the incidence of unemployment was substantially higher among migrants than among those who remained in the same area. The duration of unemployment, on the other hand, was actually slightly lower for migrants than for nonmigrants, but the difference is nonsignificant when expressed as a ratio to number of weeks in the labor force.

The variation in unemployment experience by occupation is virtually identical to that described for the younger group of women. The industrial pattern is also similar so far as the incidence of unemployment is concerned, with women in government and finance being least likely to have experienced joblessness. With respect to duration of unemployment, it is true of the older cohort, as it was of the younger, that industrial differences in cumulative weeks of duration appear to reflect at least in part corresponding differences in degree of labor market exposure.

Length of service with the 1967 employer (or most recent previous one) bears a consistent inverse relationship with the incidence of unemployment, but no consistent relationship with duration. Interfirm mobility during the decade is even more strongly related to the likelihood of experiencing some unemployment. Other things equal, only about one-fourth of the women who were with the same employer in 1967 and 1977 experienced any unemployment, while this was true of one-half of those who had changed employers.

By and large the two psychological variables bear the expected relationships with unemployment experience, but the differences are not always statistically significant. Women with high commitment to the work ethic had lower ratios of weeks unemployed to weeks in the labor force than women with low commitment. With regard to incidence and both measures of duration, "internal" women had more favorable records than the "externals," and the difference becomes significant (at the .10 level) for the relative duration measure.

For this cohort of women, the behavior of the measure of number of years with less than full labor market participation is especially intriguing and demonstrates the importance of measuring women's long term unemployment experience in relation to the extent of their labor force exposure. To illustrate, this variable bears a relationship to the incidence of unemployment that is positive, highly significant, and, except for the last category, monotonic. On the other hand, the cumulative duration of unemployment expressed in weeks bears just the opposite relationship to the years-of-nonparticipation variable. Other things equal, women with no periods out of the labor force had an average duration of 28 weeks, while those with periods of nonparticipation in six or seven years had an average duration of only 16 weeks.

This, of course, reflects the fact that women with less constant labor force exposure have less potential for unemployment. Finally, however, when duration of unemployment is measured as a percentage of weeks in the labor force (and thus holds potential for unemployment constant) a strong positive relationship is evident. Women who were out of the labor force for some portion of each of six or seven years had an unemployment ratio twice as large as those with no periods of nonparticipation. To sum all of this up, women with irregular labor force participation are more likely than others to experience some unemployment over, say, a decade. Of those who do suffer unemployment, those with irregular attachments will be unemployed for fewer weeks because of their more limited labor force exposure. However, relative to the amount of time they spend in the labor force, the more irregular the labor force attachment, the greater the amount of unemployment.

Summary

The relationships of almost a score of variables with three measures of unemployment for four age-sex cohorts are not easy to summarize systematically. Tables 7 and 8 attempt to do this, but some precision is admittedly lost in the condensation. Perhaps the most important generalization is that a considerable amount of the variation in unemployment experience over a decade remains unexplained by the independent variables, even though some of them (e.g., interfirm mobility) are almost inevitably related at least to the incidence of unemployment. Adjusted R^2s range between .09 and .45. They reach levels over .25, however, only for the relative duration variable among the two cohorts of women, and this results from the almost definitional relationship between the dependent variable and one of the independent variables (number of years with less than 52 weeks in the labor force).

Table 7
Summary of MCA Results for Men: Relationship Between Explanatory Variables and Three Measures of Unemployment Experience[a]

Characteristic	Age 26-34			Age 55-69		
	Incidence	Duration, weeks	Duration, ratio	Incidence	Duration, weeks	Duration, ratio
Black	+**	+**	+**	0	0	0
Age	0	0	0	0	0	0
Married 1966 and 1976	-**	-*	-*	-+	-	-+
Married 1966, not married 1976	n.a.	n.a.	n.a.	0	0	0
Health limitation, 1966 and/or 1976	+	+	+	+	+	+
Years of schooling	-**	-**	-**b	n.a.	n.a.	n.a.
Training outside school	0	1	1	0	0	0
High local unemployment rate, 1966[c]	+*	0	0	+	++	+
Blue collar employment	+**	+*	+*	+**	+	+
Government employment 1966 and 1976	-**	d	d	-**	-	-
Construction worker, 1966	+**	+**	+**	+**	+**	+**
Tenure in current or most recent job, 1966	-**	-*	-+	-**	0	0
Same employer, 1966 and 1976	-**	-**	-**	-**	-**	-**
Retired from "regular" job	n.a.	n.a.	n.a.	+**	+*	+*
High work commitment[e]	0	0	0	-+	-+	-+

Internal locus of control[f]	−	−	−	−+	−	−
Had military service 1966-1976	0	+*	+*	n.a.	n.a.	n.a.
Number of years with less than 52 weeks in labor force	+**	0	0	+**	−+	0
R^2	.26	.15	.16	.25	.21	.20

a. A positive relationship is indicated by a +, a negative relationship by a −, and a nonsignificant relationship by a 0. Levels of significance are indicated by ** ($\alpha = .01$), * ($\alpha = .05$) and + ($\alpha = .10$). Occasionally (e.g., health) a relationship that is systematic is shown as positive or negative even if nonsignificant. In a few cases a variable is significant but manifests a relationship that is irregular and inexplicable. These are designated by an I.

b. Except for persons with 13-15 years of education.

c. Nonmigrants only.

d. Too few cases for reliable estimate.

e. See text footnote 11.

f. See text footnote 12.

Table 8
Summary of MCA Results for Women: Relationship Between Explanatory Variables and Three Measures of Unemployment Experience[a]

Characteristic	Age 26-34			Age 40-54		
	Incidence	Duration, weeks	Duration, ratio	Incidence	Duration, weeks	Duration, ratio
Black	+**	+**	+**	+**	++	0
Age	-**	+**	+**	-**	0	I+
Married 1966 and 1976[b]	-+	-**	-*	-**	0	0
Married 1966, not married 1976[b]	+	+	+	+*	0	0
Health limitation, 1966 and/or 1976[b]	+**	+	+*	0	0	I*
Years of schooling	-**	-**	-**	-**c	-**d	I**
Training outside school	I+	0	I+	0	I**	+
High local unemployment rate, 1966[b,e]	+*	0	0	+	+	+
Blue collar employment	+**	+**	+**	+**	+**	0
Government employment 1966 and 1976	-*	0	0	-*	++	-
Finance worker, 1966[b]	-	0	0	-**	-*	-
Tenure in current or most recent job, 1966[b]	-**	0	0	-*	I**	I*
Same employer, 1966 and 1976[b]	-**	0	+	-**	-+	0
High work commitment[f]	0	+**	0	0	0	-**
Internal locus of control[g]	-	-	-	-	-	-+

Number of years with less than 52 weeks in labor force	+**	0	+**	+**	-**	+**
R²	.15	.09	.42	.16	.10	.45

a. A positive relationship is indicated by a +, a negative relationship by a −, and a nonsignificant relationship by a 0. Levels of significance are indicated by ** ($\alpha = .01$), * ($\alpha = .05$) and + ($\alpha = .10$). Occasionally (e.g., health) a relationship that is systematic is shown as positive or negative even if nonsignificant. In a few cases a variable is significant but manifests a relationship that is irregular and inexplicable. These are designated by an I.

b. The years 1966 and 1976 are used to designate the beginning and end of the decade under review for each cohort, even though the actual dates for the women are 1967-1977 for the older cohort and 1968-1978 for the younger.

c. Except for persons with 13-15 years of education.

d. Except for persons with 16 or more years of education.

e. Nonmigrants only.

f. See text footnote 10.

g. See text footnote 11.

Among the strongest and most consistent relationships across the several cohorts are educational attainment, occupational and industrial affiliation, interfirm mobility, and tenure in the job held at the beginning of the decade. With only a few anomalies, there is a highly significant inverse relationship between the amount of education a person has and the likelihood of unemployment as well as its cumulative duration over a decade among those who experience it. Perhaps the most noteworthy "anomaly" is the fact that middle-aged female college graduates, other things equal, experienced more unemployment than any other educational category relative to the amount of time they spent in the labor force.

Even controlling for educational attainment (except in the case of the older group of men, where the variable was not included) and all of the other variables in the analysis, blue-collar workers invariably suffered a higher incidence as well as a longer duration of unemployment over the decade than white-collar workers. Government workers, both male and female, fared significantly better than those in the private sector. Within the private sector, male construction workers had considerably more unemployment and female workers in finance, insurance and real estate considerably less than their average counterparts.

Men and women who had relatively short tenure in their jobs at the beginning of the decade were considerably more likely than those with longer service to experience some unemployment, although duration of unemployment was inversely related to tenure only in the case of the younger cohort of men. Workers who remained with the same employer over the decade were invariably less likely to have experienced unemployment than those who changed, and the nonchangers, generally speaking, also experienced shorter cumulative durations when they became unemployed. Those who lived continuously in areas with high unemployment rates at the beginning of the decade had a higher-than-average probability of experiencing unemployment. Average durations tended also to be higher for these groups in the case of the older cohorts of men and women.

Among the older cohort of men, the gross differences in unemployment experience between whites and blacks disappear when other factors are controlled. In the three other cohorts, however, highly significant net differences remain in the incidence of unemployment, and average duration is also significantly higher for blacks than for whites in the younger groups of males and females. Being married significantly decreases the probability of unemployment for young men, and also is associated with shorter duration among those who become unemployed. These tendencies are also evident, although to a much smaller degree, among the older group of men and young women. Marital dissolution during the decade is associated with somewhat higher incidences of unemployment among both cohorts of women and with a higher duration among the younger group. Although it rarely achieves a level of statistical significance, good health appears to be associated with a lower incidence and duration of unemployment in all of the cohorts except the older women.

The two social psychological variables exhibit, at best, a weak relationship with unemployment experience. However, individuals who believe that what happens to them is largely a function of factors beyond their control ("externals") tend to be more likely to experience unemployment and to have longer cumulative durations than "internals."

Among the younger group of men, veteran status is associated with longer cumulative durations of unemployment. Among the older cohort, retirement during the decade is associated with both a higher incidence and a longer cumulative duration. Regular labor force participation (as measured by the number of years in which there was full-year participation) is in all cases related to a below-average incidence of unemployment. Among the two cohorts of women, it bears a strong positive relationship with the ratio of weeks unemployed to weeks in the labor force.

Chronic Unemployment and Average Hourly Earnings

4

Do individuals with substantial unemployment over a decade suffer a relative loss of earning capacity as well as the loss of earnings that is directly attributable to their periods of joblessness? To pursue this question, multiple regressions have been performed in which average hourly earnings at the end of the decade are regressed on unemployment experience during the decade, controlling for the level of average hourly earnings at the beginning of the period and a series of other variables that would be expected to be correlated with both unemployment experience and change in average hourly earnings. For all four cohorts these control variables include race, cumulative number of weeks out of the labor force, the acquisition of training during the decade, migration, and change in health. For the young men and young women, change in education during the decade is also included, while for the two female cohorts, additional control variables are change in marital status and the presence of children in the household. A number of additional characteristics are, of course, related to earnings, but their influence is intended to be captured by the inclusion in each equation of the initial level of earnings.

Unemployment experience is represented by the inclusion of two dummy variables, one representing moderate unemployment during the decade (1-65 weeks); the other, chronic unemployment (66 or more weeks). Those with no unemployment during the decade are the reference group. The coefficient of each of the unemployment variables, in other words, measures the impact of that level of unemployment on the change in average hourly earnings during the decade, other things being equal. For each cohort the analysis is confined to those individuals who were employed as wage and salary workers in the survey weeks of 1966 and 1976 and for whom information was available for all variables. An additional requirement for inclusion in the case of the older group of men was that they never reported themselves as having retired.

The complete regression results are shown in appendix tables A-7 and A-8, while table 9 reproduces the regression coefficients for the unemployment variables. The influence of unemployment on the wage gain over the decade for the younger cohorts of men and women is dramatic. Other things equal (including the wage at the beginning of the decade), young men with moderate unemployment earned 47 cents less per hour in 1976 and those with chronic unemployment earned $1.43 less per hour than men who experienced no unemployment during the decade. In the case of the young women, the wage penalties attaching to unemployment were of the same order of magnitude—43 cents per hour for those with moderate unemployment and $1.86 per hour for the chronically unemployed. These differences are all highly significant. In the case of the two older cohorts the pattern is similar, but much less pronounced. For the men, hourly earnings in 1976 for those who suffered moderate unemployment were 25 cents below those of men with no unemployment, and the corresponding differential for the chronically unemployed was 73 cents, differences that achieve significance at the 10 percent level in a one-tail test. For the older cohort of women the corresponding figures were 40 cents for the moderately unemployed and 32 cents for the chronically unemployed, only the former of which is statistically significant.

Table 9
Change in Average Hourly Earnings Over Decade for Persons with Moderate and Chronic Unemployment Relative to Those with No Unemployment, by Cohort
(Regression Coefficients in Cents Per Hour)

Sex and age (1976)	n	Moderate (1-65 weeks)	Chronic (65+ weeks)
Males 26-34	920	-47**	-143**
Males 55-69	1176	-25+	-73+
Females 26-34	698	-43*	-186**
Females 40-54	1092	-40**	-32

Source: Appendix tables A-7 and A-8.
**Significant at $\alpha = .01$, 1-tail test.
*Significant at $\alpha = .05$, 1-tail test.
+ Significant at $\alpha = .10$, 1-tail test.

It seems legitimate to conclude that unemployment—particularly when it is prolonged—impedes normal wage progression as individuals are forced into lower-paying jobs, and that this phenomenon is especially pronounced among young women and men who are in the process of establishing their careers.

The Anatomy of
Chronic Unemployment   5

The group that has been referred to in previous sections as the "chronically unemployed" consists of 430 sample cases. The detailed work history over the entire decade of each of these persons has been examined to see what additional light such information sheds on the phenomenon of protracted and/or repeated unemployment. In this section, a number of case histories will be presented which will at least make more human and personal the bare statistical data that have been presented thus far. Before describing these illustrative cases, however, and as a means of selecting them, it will be useful to examine the distribution of the chronically unemployed according to the extent of their unemployment and labor force participation during the decade under review.

Distribution of Unemployment and Absence from Labor Force

To begin with, it is interesting that the distribution of chronic unemployment over the years of the decade is remarkably similar within each of the cohorts to the distribution of total unemployment, both reflecting variations in general labor market conditions as measured by the national unemployment rate. Table 10 shows for each NLS survey year (1) the national unemployment rate as reported by the

Table 10
National Unemployment Rate[a] and Percent Distribution of Total Number of Weeks of All Unemployment and of Chronic Unemployment, by Year, for Four NLS Cohorts, 1967-1978

	U.S. unemployment rate	Percent distribution of weeks of unemployment, NLS							
		Men				Women			
		26-34		55-69		26-34		40-54	
Year[b]		All	Chronic	All	Chronic	All	Chronic	All	Chronic
1967	3.8	8.9	7.8	8.4	8.0	(c)	(c)	(c)	(c)
1968	3.6	6.9	9.2	8.8	8.4	(c)	(c)	8.6	8.5
1969	3.5	7.5	6.8	7.1	7.8	10.0	8.7	9.1	7.3
1970	4.9	17.8	11.2	8.3	9.3	10.1	9.3	12.3	13.8
1971	5.9	14.8	13.2	8.3	9.3	15.8	12.0	12.3	13.8
1972	5.6	(c)	(c)	(c)	(c)	15.0	14.0	13.5	12.7
1973	4.9	7.3	9.1	10.0	11.6	11.9	10.8	(c)	(c)
1974	5.6	(c)	(c)	(c)	(c)	(c)	(c)	10.5	8.1
1975	8.5	20.2	20.0	21.5	20.2	12.2	14.5	(c)	(c)
1976	7.7	16.5	22.6	27.6	25.3	(c)	(c)	21.3	23.2
1977	7.0	(c)	(c)	(c)	(c)	14.2	17.4	12.4	12.6
1978	6.0	(c)	(c)	(c)	(c)	10.8	13.4	(c)	(c)
Total	-	100.0	100.0	100.0	100.0	100.0	100.0	100.0	100.0

a. Unemployment rates from *Employment and Training Report of the President*, 1980.

b. Calendar year for unemployment rates. Year of NLS surveys for NLS data, which relates to 12-month period preceding survey date. For older men and older women, number of weeks of unemployment reported in 1971 covered a 24-month period. This was divided equally between 1970 and 1971. See text footnote 16.

c. Not included in data.

Current Population Survey, and, for each cohort, the proportion of (2) all the weeks of unemployment and (3) all the weeks of chronic unemployment during the decade that were reported in that survey year.[16]

The 3-year period 1967-1969, when the annual unemployment rate for the nation remained under 4 percent, accounted for slightly under one-fourth of all weeks of unemployment during the decade reported by the two cohorts of males and a virtually identical proportion of all weeks of unemployment reported by the chronically unemployed males. In contrast, almost half of all the weeks of both total and chronic unemployment among the older men occurred in only the two years 1975 and 1976, when unemployment peaked at 8.5 and 7.7 percent, respectively. Among the younger men the proportion of total unemployment in these two years stood at 37 percent, and the proportion of chronic unemployment at 43 percent. While the same generalizations apply to the two female cohorts, the patterns are somewhat less pronounced, reflecting the lesser cyclical sensitivity of female than of male unemployment.[17]

To be included among the chronically unemployed, a worker had to have the equivalent of at least one-and-one-fourth years of unemployment during the eight years for which data are available. Table 11 shows that there was substantial variation in the extent of unemployment among this group. While between three-tenths and four-tenths of the several cohorts had no more than 1.5 years of involuntary idleness, one-fifth of the two male and the older female groups, and one-seventh of the younger women, were unemployed for periods cumulating to at least 2.25 years. The two younger groups had the largest proportions at the low end of the distribution.

Discontinuous labor force participation has been shown to be associated with both the incidence and duration of unemployment in the case of all four cohorts. Nevertheless, one-fifth of the chronically unemployed young men and one-third of the older group had not absented themselves from the labor force for as long as a calendar week during the entire period under review, while one-half and two-thirds, respectively, had not been out for as long as one-half year in all (table 12). In a large majority of male cases, absence from the labor force occurred in no more than two of the periods covered by the data (table 13). At the other extreme, about 6 or 7 percent reported a cumulative total of at least two years of no labor market activity.

Table 11
Percent Distribution of the Chronically Unemployed, by Cumulative Number of Weeks of Unemployment Over Preceding Decade and by Cohort, 1976[a]

Number of weeks	Men 26-34	Men 55-69	Women 26-34	Women 40-54
66-78	38	29	40	32
79-91	23	25	21	24
92-104	11	12	18	16
105-117	8	14	7	8
118 or more	21	20	13	19
Total	100	100	100	100
n	66	92	143	129

a. See footnote a, table 1.

As would be expected, the pattern among the chronically unemployed women was much different. Only 6 percent of the younger group and 11 percent of the older group had been out of the labor force for less than half a year; about one-half and three-tenths, respectively, had cumulative absences of at least three years (table 12). A majority of the women in each age group reported absences from the labor force in at least four of the years covered by the data (table 13). This proportion was 53 percent among the older group, but as high as 82 percent among the younger group, reflecting both the higher school attendance and fertility rates of the latter.[18]

Table 12
Percent Distribution of the Chronically Unemployed, by Cumulative Number of Weeks Out of Labor Force Over Preceding Decade and by Cohort, 1976[a,b]

Number of weeks	Men 26-34	Men 55-69	Women 26-34	Women 40-54
0	18	32	0	3
1-25	32	34	6	8
26-51	15	8	6	13
52-77	20	14	5	11
78-103	9	5	10	12
104-155	3	5	24	20
156-207	3	2	25	13
208-259	0	0	12	9
260 or more	0	0	11	9
Total	100	100	100	100
n	66	92	143	129

a. See footnote a, table 1.

b. Distribution based on minimum estimates, since no imputations were made (as were in the case of unemployment) for years in which information was missing.

46

Table 13
Percent Distribution of Chronically Unemployed, by Number of Years of Less than Continuous (52 weeks) Labor Force Participation Over Preceding Decade, and by Cohort, 1976[a]

Number of survey years[b] with 1 or more weeks out of labor force	Men 26-34	Men 55-69	Women 26-34	Women 40-54
0	18	32	0	3
1	30	29	5	7
2	11	25	4	14
3	26	11	10	22
4	11	3	17	25
5	3	0	22	19
6 or more	2	0	43	9
Total	100	100	100	100
n	66	92	143	129

a. Percentages may not add to 100 because of rounding. Data cover only 8 years ending in 1976 for the males, in 1977 for the older group of women, and in 1978 for the younger group of women.

b. Maximum is 8 for the young men and women but only 7 for the older cohorts because in the 1971 survey of the latter groups, number of weeks out of the labor force was obtained for the preceding 24 months with no differentiation according to time period.

Case Studies

Careful scrutiny of the 430 records of chronic unemployment suggests that "prototypical cases" is not really an appropriate term for referring to any reasonably limited subset that might be drawn for illustrative purposes. Indeed, the most striking aspect of the detailed data is the rich variety of patterns that is revealed. There is an almost infinite number of ways in which one can experience a total of one-and-one-fourth or more years of unemployment over a decade! Studying the detailed records also produces a sense of frustration; while they do indeed yield insights that the bare statistics do not afford, they leave a great deal unexplained. The kinds of data produced by a large scale survey such as the NLS permit descriptions of events in a respondent's life, but little in the way of interpretations. After examining a computer printout of the relevant information for an individual, one generally longs for an opportunity to talk to her or him for an account of why things happened as they did and how this respondent reacted.

Appendix tables A-9 to A-12 summarize important aspects of the labor market experience of 10 individuals within each cohort who suffered chronic unemployment. As already indicated, they cannot purport to be representative in a statistical sense; they do however, illustrate the range of variability. For each cohort about half of the cases were chosen to represent each extreme of the continuum of labor market participation.

Men 26 to 34. As is well known, and as earlier sections of this study have documented, affiliation with the construction industry substantially increases the probability of unemployment. Of the 66 cases of chronic unemployment among the younger group of men, 10 began the decade in construction. Yet, it must be remembered that the total sample included about 30 young men in the same industrial category who experienced no unemployment during the period. Moreover, as Cases 1 and 2 (appendix table A-9) illustrate, even within construction the pattern of chronic unemployment may vary widely. Case 2, a road machinery operator, served with five different employers[19] and accumulated a total of 147 weeks of unemployment that were distributed rather evenly among the eight years covered by the data. In contrast, Case 1, a carpenter, experienced virtually no unemployment until 1975 when he reported 52 weeks of joblessness that extended an additional 25 weeks into the next 12-month period. By the time of the 1976 survey, he was again employed in construction, but as a laborer rather than a craftsman.

Cases 3, 4, and 5 also illustrate quite different patterns, but outside the construction industry. Especially marked is the difference between Cases 4 and 5. The first of these is a

30-year-old black man who had a high school diploma at the beginning of the decade and later completed one year of college. From 1966 through 1973 he was continuously employed at the same printing establishment, first as an operative, then as a bookbinder, next as an apprentice printer, and finally as a bookbinder again in 1973. He lost his job,[20] however, and was unemployed in 1975, reporting 35 weeks of unemployment for the preceding 12-month period. He remained unemployed for 40 weeks during the ensuing 12 months but, happily, had by 1976 found a job in a different firm as an office manager.

In contrast to the relative immobility of this individual, Case 5 is a white high school dropout, three years older, who worked for at least six different employers during the decade and whose occupational assignments included fountain worker (1966), auto mechanic (1967) and truck driver. Most of his job changing was voluntary and was accompanied by some unemployment, cumulating to 53 weeks by the time of the 1975 survey. The most prolonged spell (45 weeks), however, occurred during the ensuing 12 months. By the time of the 1976 survey he was reemployed as a truck driver in the transportation industry.

Cases 6-10 are all individuals who spent at least half a year during the decade outside the labor force, ranging from exactly 26 weeks (Cases 8 and 10) to 128 weeks (Case 7). Two of these individuals reported work-limiting health problems either in 1966 (Case 10) or 1976 (Case 9). Cases 6 and 9 had additional schooling during the decade, although neither reported himself as being out of the labor force at the time of any of the nine surveys between 1966 and 1976. Most members of this group had numerous employers during the decade—as many as eight for Case 6, a 28-year-old black man with seven years of schooling who started the decade as a farm laborer and ended as a laborer with a construction firm.

Men 55 to 69 (table A-10). The data for the older cohort of men provide additional evidence of the diversity of the pattern of chronic unemployment in the construction industry. Cases 14 and 15 are both individuals whose only occupations during the decade were as craftsmen in construction. The former reported some unemployment in each survey year. In contrast, the latter's unemployment occurred almost entirely between 1973 and 1976. Unlike these two individuals, who spent the entire decade in construction despite considerable unemployment, Case 16 left the industry and succeeded in finding more steady employment. By 1971 he had obtained work as a motorman in the mining industry. From then until the 1976 survey he experienced no unemployment and rose to the position of foreman with the company.

Quite atypical of the chronically unemployed older men are Cases 12 and 13, both of whom had only one employer during the entire decade. The latter, a 62-year-old white man with an elementary school education, was a loom fixer with 20 years of service in a textile manufacturing firm, with no recorded unemployment through the 1973 survey. He lost his job in 1974, however, and even by 1976 had been unsuccessful in finding work. The other individual with only one employer began the decade as a manager in a metal manufacturing firm, where he had been employed for nine years, and reported no unemployment through the 1973 survey. At the time of the 1975 survey he was employed at the same firm, but had experienced a layoff of 19 weeks. In 1976 he reported himself as unemployed, with 47 weeks of joblessness in the previous twelve months.

In contrast to these two men, Case 11 represents considerably mobility. A 60-year-old black man with 11 years of education, he had been employed in 1966 as a decorator in a business service firm. In each succeeding survey year through 1969 he reported both a different employer and a different occupation, serving in turn as an operative, a janitor, and a guard. The latter position he continued to hold in 1971, but lost it in 1973, following which he accumulated all of his 66 weeks of unemployment.

None of the chronically unemployed older men discussed thus far was out of the labor force for as many as 12 weeks (cumulatively) over the entire decade. Four of the cases shown in table A-10, however, had absented themselves from the labor force for a total of at least half a year, and two of these were out for more than a year. One (Case 19) reported a work-limiting health problem in 1966 and two (Cases 17 and 20) reported such a condition in 1976. The individual in this group who reported no health problems is a 57-year-old man with nine years of education who began the decade as a millwright in a food manufacturing plant where he had 20 years of service. By the 1967 survey date he had retired, and reported that he had been seeking work for 20 weeks. In 1969 and at each subsequent survey date he was working, generally as a guard, but in 1971 as a janitor, a different employer in each year. Over that entire period there were 68 weeks out of the labor force, 38 weeks of unemployment.

Women 26 to 34. It is hardly surprising that all three of the women shown in table A-11 who were out of the labor force for fewer than 10 weeks over the decade were unmarried at the time of the 1968 and 1978 surveys (Cases 21, 22, and 25). Although each of these experienced substantial unemployment, ranging between 72 and 128 weeks, their patterns were quite different. Case 21, a 28-year-old white woman, escaped unemployment only in the 12-month period preceding the 1978 survey. In every other year there were periods of joblessness ranging between 6 and 36 weeks, although she had only three employers over the 10-year period. In contrast, virtually all of the unemployment of Case 25 was concentrated in the 12 months prior to the 1971 survey. Aside from that extended spell, this 29-year-old black woman had a total of only 21 weeks of joblessness. However, she worked for a series of different employers during the decade, and made a shift from white-collar to blue-collar work after her extended spell of unemployment.

Five of the women shown in table A-11 had extensive withdrawals from the labor force, ranging from 146 to 294 weeks. All of them had at least one preschool-age child in their care at some time during the decade. Their patterns of unemployment vary considerably. For instance, over two-thirds of the total unemployment reported by Case 28, a 31-year-old white medical technician, was reported in the single survey year 1977. Between 1970 and that time, there had been limited work activity, but no extended periods of job seeking. In 1977, however, her lack of success during the 52-week search for work apparently induced her to give up, for in 1978 she was not looking for work at the time of the survey and had been out of the labor force for the entire year.

Case 30 represents one in which unemployment was more evenly distributed over the years. This 27-year-old black woman was unemployed in every survey week but one between 1968 and 1973 and reported a total of 95 weeks of joblessness during that period. Except in 1973 when she worked for a total of about 40 weeks as a salesperson, there was virtually no employment during this period. Beginning in 1975, she was out of the labor force continuously.

Women 40 to 54. Three of the women shown in table A-12 reported no absences from the labor force during the entire decade. All of these were married, with school-age children at the beginning of the decade, but none under 16 at the end. For one of these chronically unemployed women, joblessness was concentrated in the early part of the decade (Case 35); in a second it occurred in the final two years (Case 34); and in the third it was distributed fairly evenly throughout the 10-year period (Case 33). This woman was unique in having had only one job during the entire decade. She served as an operative, but suffered repeated layoffs that cumulated to 158 weeks.

In terms of their marital and family status, the women with substantial periods out of the labor force are basically indistinguishable from those that have already been described. All but one were married in both 1976 and 1977, the one exception having been separated in the former year and widowed by the latter. All, however, had school-age children in 1967, but none under 16 by 1977. A 48-year-old white woman (Case 36), whose previous work experience had been as a private household worker, was out of the labor force at the time of the initial survey in 1967 and for almost all of the two ensuing years. By the 1971 survey date, however, she had spent a total of 88 weeks looking for work before finding a job as a cook. From that point there was no further withdrawal from the labor force, but a total of 63 weeks of unemployment with at least one change of employer.

In contrast to this woman, a 51-year-old white woman (Case 37) had her labor force attachment and her unemployment concentrated in the first part of the decade. A total of 123 weeks of unemployment were reported between the surveys of 1968 and 1971, after which the woman was almost continuously out of the labor force. The limited employment that she had during the decade was exclusively in semi-skilled blue-collar work.

The more than 90 weeks of unemployment experienced by Case 39, a 53-year-old white woman, all occurred during the first and the last two years of the decade. In both 1967 and 1968 she was employed as a stewardess, but reported eight weeks of unemployment in the 1967 survey and 20 weeks in 1968. In the surveys between 1969 and 1974 no unemployment was reported, but there were substantial periods out of the labor force—a total of 147 weeks. The limited employment activity that recurred over this period was as a stewardess, then as a waitress, and finally as a secretary. At the time of both the 1975 and 1976 surveys, the woman was seeking work and had registered a total of 46 weeks of unemployment in the first of these periods and 26 in the second. The work that she had was as a clerical worker.

Summary and Conclusions

6

Taking advantage of longitudinal data, this paper has analyzed the unemployment experience during a recent 10-year period of four subsets of the U.S. labor force: men who at the end of the decade were 26-34 and 55-69 and women who were 26-34 and 40-54. To be included in the analysis, men had to have spent some part of each year in the labor force; women were included if they were in the labor force at any time during the decade. Although the data for each group span 10 years, information on unemployment is available in each case for only 8 years; the data therefore understate both the incidence and the amount of unemployment that occurred over the 10-year period for these four groups. The following statements are a distillation of the principal findings.

1. Large proportions of individuals with labor force exposure are subject to some unemployment over a 10-year period—majorities of young men and women and three or four out of ten of the older groups.

2. Unemployment experience over a decade varies substantially among the four age-sex cohorts. Its incidence is highest among the young women (68 percent) and lowest among the older group of men (29 percent). However, among those who experience

unemployment, the average cumulative duration is highest among the older men (31 weeks); for each of the other three cohorts it falls in the narrow range of 20-24 weeks.

3. The unemployment experience of women relative to that of men becomes worse when its duration is measured in relation to number of weeks in the labor force. That ratio is 8 and 9 percent for the younger and older females; 6 and 8 percent for the younger and older males.

4. Within each cohort, unemployment is very unequally distributed. In each case, the 10 percent of the unemployed who had the longest cumulative duration accounted for between 35 and 40 percent of all the weeks of unemployment that occurred during the decade under review. When those with no unemployment are also considered, the 5 percent of all individuals with the most unemployment account for over one-half of all unemployment among the older males and between 29 and 45 percent in the other three cohorts.

5. Those with at least 1.25 years of unemployment (cumulative durations of 66 or more weeks) have been quite arbitrarily designated as the "chronically unemployed." This group represents only a tiny fraction of each cohort (3-5 percent), yet accounts for as much as one-fifth of all weeks of unemployment experienced by the young women, one-third of the unemployment of the young men and older women, and one-half of that of the older men.

6. Within the chronically unemployed group there is considerable variation in the exent of unemployment. As many as 118 weeks of unemployment were recorded by one-fifth of each cohort except the young women, among whom the proportion was 13 percent.

7. Both total unemployment and chronic unemployment are distributed similarly across the eight years covered by the data. Years in which the national unemployment rate was high accounted for disproportionately high percentages of all weeks of unemployment and of all weeks of chronic unemployment.

8. Unemployment means not only the lost earnings attributable directly to the periods of idleness, but leads also to long term reductions in earning capacity. This is particularly true among young men and women. For example, the 1976 average hourly earnings of young men with moderate unemployment were 47 cents lower, and those with chronic unemployment $1.43 lower, than the earnings of comparable men with no unemployment during the decade. Similar but less pronounced patterns prevail among the older men and women.

9. Multivariate analysis uncovered a number of human capital and employment characteristics that bear strong relationships with the incidence and/or duration of unemployment among all four cohorts. Among the strongest and most consistent are educational attainment, occupational and industrial affiliation, interfirm mobility, and tenure in the job held at the beginning of the decade. Generally speaking, with female college graduates being a notable exception, the amount of education a person has is inversely related both to the likelihood of unemployment and its cumulative duration if it occurs. Blue-collar workers suffer a higher incidence and longer duration than white-collar workers. Government workers fare better than private wage and salary workers. Employment in certain industries increases or decreases the risk of unemployment: construction is particularly unfavorable for males; finance, insurance and real estate is particularly favorable for women. Short

tenure in the job held at the beginning of the decade increases the likelihood of unemployment. Movement among employers is associated with unemployment, sometimes as cause and sometimes as effect. Involuntary separations from the earliest job are particularly likely to eventuate in chronic unemployment.

10. There is also evidence of relationships between certain personal characteristics and unemployment experience. Of these, race has by all odds the most pronounced effect. When other factors are controlled, there remains a highly significant racial difference, unfavorable to blacks, in both the incidence and duration of unemployment in three of the four cohorts. Only in the case of the older males do racial differences melt away when other factors are controlled. Marital status also makes a difference. Unmarried males and young women have less favorable unemployment experience than their married counterparts. Among both groups of women, marital dissolution is associated with more unemployment. Although the evidence is considerably less strong, it appears that poor health and lack of initiative (as reflected in the Rotter I-E scale) each contribute to increased unemployment.

11. The foregoing factors, together with several others that were found to be related to the incidence and/or duration of unemployment in the case of one or more cohorts, account for only small proportions (between 10 and 25 percent)[21] of the total variation in unemployment experience. Like other studies of factors associated with the incidence or duration of unemployment, this one leaves most of the variability unaccounted for. A substantial amount of unemployment experience appears to result either from simply being in the wrong place at the wrong time, or from personality characteristics that generally go unmeasured.

12. Case studies of the chronically unemployed underscore dramatically the variability that characterizes chronic unemployment. For men and women alike it occurs among those with constant and those with little and irregular labor force exposure; among white-collar and blue-collar workers; among job hoppers and those with relatively stable ties to employers and occupations. Moreover, it occurs in almost every conceivable temporal pattern—concentrated at the beginning or the middle or end of the decade or scattered indiscriminately among the 10 years. There is clearly no singular explanation for the phenomenon.

It is hard to decide whether to be encouraged or discouraged by these findings. From an egalitarian perspective, the extreme concentration of the economic and psychological burdens of unemployment among relatively small proportions of labor market participants is cause for concern. Moreover, the evidence that unemployment produces a deterioration of earning capacity means that measures of earnings loss during periods of unemployment understate the full economic cost of unemployment to the individual. On the brighter side, the similarity in the temporal distributions of total and chronic unemployment, and the fact that both are similarly responsive to variations in general economic conditions, tend to dispel the more extreme pessimistic interpretations of structural unemployment.

While the findings do not lead to a grand reinterpretation of the problem of unemployment, they do make suspect the modern neoclassical interpretation based on search theory, according to which all unemployment is really voluntary. A leading textbook on the economics of the labor market succinctly summarizes this view as follows:

Economists have begun to view unemployment as a form of labor market behavior that can be analyzed with the general theory of choice. Unemployed workers who are not temporarily laid off and waiting to be called back to their jobs are viewed as choosing to look for work (search) rather than to accept the best job offered at the moment or to quit active search and, by definition, withdraw from the labor force.

It then devotes seven pages to a numerical illustration of how a wealth-maximizing individual develops and executes a "search strategy."[22]

I acknowledge that all behavior (except being born and dying) is in some tautological sense inevitably a matter of choice; nevertheless, the case studies of the chronically unemployed make it quite impossible for me to maintain the mental image of a "wealth maximizer" carefully balancing the marginal costs and benefits of additional search for work. The evidence supports the verdict rendered by Robert Solow who, on the basis of a quite different kind of analysis, said in his 1979 presidential address to the American Economic Association ". . . I believe that what looks like involuntary unemployment *is* involuntary unemployment."[23]

Notes

1. In 1978, when the average unemployment rate was 6.0 percent, 15.8 percent of those in the labor force at any time during the year experienced at least a week of unemployment. At that annual rate, a random distribution of unemployment over time would imply that over 80 percent of all workers would have some unemployment over a 10-year period $(1 - [1 - .158]^{10} = .82)$.

2. In other respects the study by Corcoran and Hill (1979), based on PSID data, is the most comparable both to the Parnes-Nestel 1980 study and to the present one. It examines, among other things, the incidence and cumulative duration of unemployment among males over the decade ending in 1976, as well as the correlates of these measures. However, there are differences in the data and methods of analysis: (a) PSID data rely on a less precise measure of unemployment than the NLS data, for they do not ascertain whether the respondent was actually seeking work during the reported periods of "unemployment" and, in some years, include time lost from striking (Corcoran and Hill, fn. 4). The NLS data use official CPS questions. (b) PSID data provide measures for each year of the decade; NLS data provide measures for only 8 years. (c) Corcoran and Hill confined their analysis to household heads 35 to 64 years of age in 1976 who were in the labor force in each year of the decade; our data are for all males 26 to 34 years old and 55 to 69 years old in 1976 who were in the labor force in each year of the decade, excluding young men who were enrolled in school in 1966. Members of the two NLS female cohorts are included if they spent at least one week of the decade in the labor force. (d) Corcoran and Hill analyzed the distribution of total unemployment in terms of hours of unemployment, while we use weeks; their measures include those with no unemployment, while ours are calculated both including and excluding persons with no unemployment. (e) Corcoran and Hill analyzed the correlates of the duration of unemployment by using a series of dichotomous dependent variables indicating the incidence of unemployment in excess of specified numbers of weeks. We use two continuous variables (number of weeks of unemployment and ratio of weeks unemployed to weeks in the labor force) for individuals who experienced any unemployment during the decade.

3. For a detailed description of the NLS data base, see Center for Human Resource Research (1982). Interviews with the older cohort of men were conducted in 1966, 1967, 1969, 1971, 1973, 1975, and 1976, and a mail survey was conducted in 1968. The younger men were inter-

viewed annually between 1966 and 1971 and in 1973, 1975, and 1976. Survey years for the older group of women were 1967, 1968 (mail), 1969, 1971, 1972, 1974, 1976, and 1977. The young women were interviewed annually between 1968 and 1973, in 1975, 1977, and 1978. In the second interview of each cohort and each subsequent one the respondent was asked a series of questions identical to those used in the March supplement of the CPS designed to ascertain how many weeks of unemployment had been experienced in the preceding 12 months (or since the 1969 interview in the case of the 1971 surveys of the older men and women).

In our 1980 study of the two groups of males, we filled out the 10-year period for each respondent by imputing to each of the nonsurvey years the average number of weeks of unemployment experienced in the survey years. This had no effect on the measured incidence of unemployment, but raised the measures of duration. For instance, in the case of the young men the mean duration of unemployment of the entire sample was 16 weeks with the imputations and 13 weeks when no imputations were made. For the older group of men, the corresponding means were 11 and 9. No such imputations have been made in the present study.

4. To illustrate with reference to the young men, when the universe is defined to include only those with labor force exposure in each year, 53 percent of the sample experienced some unemployment while the proportion is 59 percent of those in the labor force at any time during the decade, reflecting the expected influence of irregular labor force attachment on the incidence of unemployment. However, the proportion of each universe with very long cumulative durations (over 66 weeks) is identical at 5 percent. Moreover, when attention is confined to those who experienced some unemployment, identical proportions (43 percent) of both groups experienced less than 10 weeks. The mean duration of unemployment is 24 weeks when the universe is defined to include those who were in the labor force in every year and 23 weeks when it is expanded to include those who were in the labor force in any one of the years. The concentration of unemployment among those with the longest durations is also very little different as between the two universes. In the more restricted universe, those with 66 or more weeks of unemployment over the 8-year period account for 36 percent of all of the weeks of unemployment as compared with 33 percent for the less restricted universe. The interracial differences in the distribution of unemployment are virtually identical in the two universes.

The data for the other three cohorts are, if anything, even less sensitive than those of the young men to these variations in the specification of the universe. It should also be noted in appendix tables A-1 and A-2 that the measures for the younger cohorts are substantially the same for those who were not enrolled in school in any of the survey years as for the total group. Similarly, in the case of the older men, it makes very little difference in the data if one excludes those who had reported themselves as retired at any time during the decade.

5. Despite the differences in the data base and the methods of analysis that have been described (see fn. 2), the study by Corcoran and Hill (1979) has produced roughly comparable estimates of the incidence of unemployment over the decade among men 55 to 64 years of age. The NLS estimate for white men in this age range is 29 percent while the estimate by Corcoran and Hill is 36 percent. For blacks, the corresponding percentages are 37 percent (NLS) and 45 percent (PSID).

6. Of course, this statement must be qualified by virtue of the fact that labor force status for purposes of computing official unemployment rates is ascertained by a series of probing questions relating to activity in the reference week; the data here are based on the respondent's recollection of the number of weeks he or she occupied each status (employed, unemployed, out of the labor force) over a 12-month period.

7. Σ weeks unemployed $\div \Sigma$ weeks in labor force.

8. This clustering of unemployment among a small subset of the total "eligible" population has been documented by a number of studies of men, although to the best of my knowledge there have been no previous comparable studies of women. Corcoran and Hill (1979) report that about 5 percent of the 35-64-year-old men in 1976 accounted for about 50 percent of all unemployment in the previous 10 years. Dickinson, also using PSID data, found that 4 percent of all male household heads accumulated at least 40 weeks of unemployment in the 5-year period 1967-1971. Clark and Summers (1979) reported that among NLS men 49 to 63 in 1969, 40 percent of the total unemployment over the period 1965-1968 was attributable to men who experienced 51 or more weeks of joblessness.

9. Multiple classification analysis (MCA) allows one to calculate for each category of a particular explanatory variable (for example, blacks and whites) what the incidence (or duration) of unemployment would have been had the members of the category been "average" in terms of all the other variables entering into the analysis. Differences in these "adjusted" figures among the categories of a given variable thus represent the pure or net effect of that variable, controlling for all the others in the analysis. The MCA formulation is more general than the more familiar multiple regression approach since it avoids the assumption of linearity between independent and dependent variables. The constant term in the multiple classification equation is the mean of the dependent

variable. The coefficient of each category of every explanatory variable represents a deviation from this mean and is used to calculate the "adjusted" figures shown in the tables.

10. This variable differentiates between individuals who were employed in the same firm (or self-employed status) in all survey years and those who had made at least one change of employer.

11. Respondents who were in the labor force were asked what they would do if they had enough income to live comfortably without working. Those who responded that they would work were coded as having "high commitment." Others were coded as having "low commitment."

12. A modified version of the Rotter I-E scale was used. "Internals" believe that they are largely masters of their own lives; "externals" perceive that what happens to them is largely a matter of forces over which they have little control. For a description of the scale, see Andrisani and Nestel (1975).

13. Generally speaking, the explanatory variables are the same for the four cohorts, but there are a few exceptions. In the case of the two groups of women, marital status is combined with parental status (i.e., presence or absence of children). Veteran status is included as a variable in the case of the younger cohort of men, as is retirement status for the older group. Finally, for the latter cohort, years of school completed has been omitted because its inclusion in an earlier version of the analysis showed it to be very highly correlated with occupation.

14. Even here, however, the variable is not truly exogenous in the case of the two younger cohorts since returning to school for additional education may be motivated by unsatisfactory experience in the labor market.

15. Young men who had training between 1966 and 1976 but no training prior to 1966 had shorter than average cumulative duration of unemployment, but this was not true of men who had training both prior and subsequent to 1966.

16. In interpreting the data, it should be kept in mind that the NLS data do not relate precisely to the same time periods as the CPS unemployment data and, moreover, are not invariable in this respect across cohorts. Whereas the CPS data are on a calendar year basis, the NLS data shown in table 10 are generally for the 12-month period preceding the survey date each year. These dates center around November of each year for the younger men, August for the older men, May for the older women, and March for the younger women. Thus, the NLS data for the younger cohort of men are reasonably comparable temporally to the CPS data. On the other hand, for the younger cohort of women, the

NLS data for a given year are more nearly comparable to the CPS data for the preceding year.

17. To illustrate, while the overall CPS unemployment rate rose from 5.6 percent to 8.5 percent between 1974 and 1975, the male unemployment rate rose by 3.1 percentage points as compared with 2.6 percentage points for women (calculated from U.S. Department of Labor, 1980, pp. 217-218).

18. An additional factor is artifactual: the maximum number of years that could have been recorded was seven for the older group and eight for the younger.

19. See table A-12, footnote d.

20. The data, unfortunately, do not always allow differentiation between voluntary and involuntary job separations. Phrases of this kind are used when permitted by available information.

21. The adjusted R^2 is as high as 42-45 percent for the women when the dependent variable is the ratio of weeks unemployed to weeks in the labor force, but this results from the strong association between that measure and one of the explanatory variables (number of years with less than 52 weeks of labor force exposure).

22. Fleisher and Kniesner (1980), p. 374. For a review of the literature on search theory, see Lippman and McCall (1976).

23. Solow (1979), p. 3, my italics.

Appendix Tables

Table A-1
Effect of Different Universe Specifications on Measures of Unemployment Experience: NLS Male Cohorts, 1966-1976

Cohort and universe specification	Age 26-34				Age 55-69		
	In labor force each year		In labor force at least one week during decade			In labor force at least one week during decade	
Unemployment measure	Not enrolled in school 1966	Not enrolled in school any year	Total	Not enrolled in school any year	In labor force each year	Total	Never retired
All respondents							
N	1275	1034	2722	1091	2248	3325	1853
Percent with no unemployment	47	45	41	44	71	70	73
Percent unemployed 1-9 weeks	23	25	25	24	10	12	12
Percent unemployed 66+ weeks	5	5	5	6	4	4	3
Mean weeks unemployed	13	13	14	14	9	9	8
Respondents with some unemployment							
Percent unemployed 1-9 weeks	43	44	43	42	36	38	43
Percent unemployed 66+ weeks	9	9	8	10	14	13	12
Mean weeks unemployed	24	24	23	25	31	31	30

Percent of all unemployment experienced by persons who were unemployed:

Less than 10 weeks	8	8	8	8	5	5	6
10-25 weeks	19	18	19	17	11	12	12
26-65 weeks	37	38	40	37	37	36	35
66+ weeks	36	36	33	38	47	46	48

Table A-2
Effect of Different Universe Specifications on Measures of Unemployment Experience: NLS Female Cohorts, 1967-1977[a]

Cohort and universe specification / Unemployment measure	Age 26-34			Age 40-54	
	In labor force each year	In labor force at least one week during decade		In labor force each year	n labor force In labor force at least one week during decade
		Total	Not enrolled in school any year		
All respondents					
N	1331	3031	1504	1674	3343
Percent with no unemployment	29	32	40	63	60
Percent unemployed 1-9 weeks	30	31	28	15	17
Percent unemployed 66+ weeks	3	3	3	3	3
Mean weeks unemployed	14	13	11	9	9
Respondents with some unemployment					
Percent unemployed 1-9 weeks	43	45	47	41	44
Percent unemployed 66+ weeks	5	5	4	9	9
Mean weeks unemployed	20	20	19	25	24
Percent of all unemployment experienced by persons who were unemployed:					
Less than 10 weeks	8	9	10	7	7
10-25 weeks	23	22	22	18	17
26-65 weeks	49	48	49	38	41
66+ weeks	20	21	20	38	35

a. The time period for the age group 26-34 is 1968-1978.

Table A-3

Incidence and Duration of Unemployment, 1966-1976, by Selected Characteristics: Men 26-34 in 1976 (MCA Results)

Characteristic	Percent with some unemployment			Persons with some unemployment					
					Cumulative number of weeks		Unemployment ratio[d]		
	n	Unadjusted	Adjusted	n	Unadjusted	Adjusted	Unadjusted	Adjusted	
Total sample	1275	53	53 **	726	24	24 **	6.0	6.0 **	
Race			**			**		**	
Whites	945	50	52	484	21	22	5.4	5.6	
Blacks	330	73	63	242	35	32	9.0	8.1	
Age (1976)									
26-29	417	66	55	295	23	23	6.0	5.9	
30-32	451	51	53	243	24	24	6.1	6.1	
33-34	407	44	53	188	24	24	6.0	6.1	
Marital status			**			**		**	
Married 1966 and 1976	521	44	49	244	20	20	5.1	5.2	
Not married 1966, married 1976	501	57	54	304	19	19	4.8	4.8	
Other	251	70	63	177	38	37	9.9	9.7	
Health									
No limitations	1040	51	53	577	23	23	5.9	5.8	
Limitations in 1966 and/or 1976	221	62	56	141	25	26	6.4	6.8	

Table A-3 (continued)

Characteristic	Percent with some unemployment			Persons with some unemployment				
					Cumulative number of weeks		Unemployment ratio[d]	
	n	Unadjusted	Adjusted	n	Unadjusted	Adjusted	Unadjusted	Adjusted
Training			*			*		*
None	356	61	51	228	30	25	7.8	6.4
Prior to 1966, none later	73	52	54	37	27	25	7.0	6.2
Prior to 1966 and later	319	50	54	166	22	27	5.7	6.8
None prior to 1966, some later	471	51	53	263	19	19	4.7	4.9
Local unemployment rate, 1967			*					
Nonmigrants								
3.8 percent or lower	338	46	49	167	24	24	6.0	6.2
Over 3.8 percent	364	53	52	208	24	22	6.2	5.6
Migrants	554	56	56	333	23	24	5.9	6.1
			**			**		**
Years of schooling, 1976								
Same in 1966 and 1976								
Less than 12	249	68	61	175	31	28	8.2	7.2
12	474	49	53	244	17	19	4.3	4.7
13-15	79	43	47	32	21	26	5.3	6.7
16 or more	51	21	31	10	a	a	a	a
Different in 1966 and 1976								
Less than 12	129	82	67	106	33	28	8.3	7.0
12	78	55	54	50	28	29	7.4	7.7
13-15	153	51	51	82	24	25	6.2	6.5
16 or more	53	51	51	27	14	15	3.8	3.7

71

Occupation			**			*	*	*
Same 1-digit, 1966 and 1976								
White-collar	97	30	46	26	13	17	3.4	4.2
Blue-collar	285	62	58	187	25	26	6.5	6.7
Other	59	26	43	21	a	a	a	a
Different 1-digit, 1966 and 1976								
White-collar in 1976	289	41	47	124	16	18	4.0	4.7
Blue-collar in 1976	444	68	60	310	26	24	6.5	6.2
Other in 1976	64	55	50	40	28	27	7.3	7.0
Class of worker/industry			**			**		**
Government, 1966 and 1976	65	17	38	15	a	a	a	a
Private wage and salary, 1966 and 1976								
Construction in 1966	80	77	66	60	36	35	9.1	9.0
Manufacturing in 1966	393	57	58	230	20	21	5.0	5.4
Service in 1966	355	51	51	194	25	25	6.5	6.4
Other in 1966	71	72	66	53	26	23	6.6	5.7
Other	294	50	48	164	21	21	5.4	5.3
Tenure in current or last job, 1966			**			*	+	
Less than 1 year	636	61	57	411	26	26	6.8	6.6
1-2 years	384	50	53	201	20	21	5.1	5.4
3 or more years	239	39	46	106	20	21	5.0	5.2
Mobility status			**			**		
Same employer, 1966-1976	251	23	33	61	12	15	2.9	3.7
Changed employer, 1966-1976	1018	51	58	662	25	24	6.3	6.2

Table A-3 (continued)

| Characteristic | Percent with some unemployment | | | Persons with some unemployment | | | | |
| | | | | | Cumulative number of weeks | | Unemployment ratio[d] | |
	n	Unadjusted	Adjusted	n	Unadjusted	Adjusted	Unadjusted	Adjusted
Commitment to work, 1969[b]								
High	966	50	52	518	23	24	5.8	6.0
Low	185	60	55	113	27	24	6.9	6.1
Locus of control (Rotter I-E Scale, 1968)								
Internal	452	46	52	219	20	23	5.1	5.7
External	495	57	54	301	27	25	6.9	6.4
Veteran status		**				*		*
Veteran	420	55	52	242	24	26	6.1	6.7
Nonveteran	855	52	54	484	23	22	6.0	5.6
Number of years of less than continuous labor force participation[c]		**						
None	381	36	42	151	23	23	5.4	5.6
1	402	54	54	229	22	22	5.4	5.5
2-3	400	64	60	273	25	25	6.4	6.4
4-5	85	80	73	68	29	26	7.8	7.3
6-7	7	a	a	5	a	a	a	a

R² (adjusted)	.26	.15	.16

a. Percentage not shown when base is fewer than 25 sample cases.

b. See text footnote 11.

c. I.e., less than 52 weeks.

d. (Weeks unemployed/weeks in labor force) x 100.

**F-ratio is significant at $\alpha = .01$.

*F-ratio is significant at $\alpha = .05$.

+F-ratio is significant at $\alpha = .10$.

Table A-4

Incidence and Duration of Unemployment, 1966-1976, by Selected Characteristics: Men 55-69 in 1976 (MCA Results)

Characteristic	Percent with some unemployment			Persons with some unemployment				
					Cumulative number of weeks		Unemployment ratio^c	
	n	Unadjusted	Adjusted	n	Unadjusted	Adjusted	Unadjusted	Adjusted
Total sample	2248	29	29**	687	31	31**	7.9	7.9**
Race								
Whites	1652	28	29	465	31	31	7.9	8.0
Blacks	596	37	30	222	31	28	8.5	7.5
Age (1976)								
55-59	1113	29	29	345	31	30	7.9	7.9
60-64	810	30	30	255	31	32	7.8	8.0
65-69	325	24	25	87	29	28	8.0	7.6
Marital status								
Married 1966 and 1976	1878	28	+ 28	543	30	30	7.6	+ 7.6
Married 1966, not married 1976	153	32	28	57	30	30	8.1	8.1
Other	214	40	36	87	36	37	9.9	10.0
Health								
No limitations	1432	27	28	412	30	30	7.4	7.7
Limitations in 1966 and/or 1976	804	31	30	266	33	33	8.6	8.4

75

							**	**
Training								
None	810	32	29	282	31	29	8.0	7.5
Prior to 1966, none later	551	29	28	163	33	32	8.5	8.3
Prior to 1966 and later	500	24	28	121	25	28	6.4	7.1
None prior to 1966, some later	325	32	32	103	30	31	7.8	8.0
Local unemployment rate, 1967								
Nonmigrants								
3.8 percent or lower	936	25	27	241	25	27	6.5	6.9
Over 3.8 percent	954	30	30	305	34	33	8.9	8.6
Migrants	281	35	30	104	32	33	8.3	8.6
Occupation		**	**					
Same 3-digit, 1966 and 1976								
White-collar	379	15	24	52	25	24	6.2	8.0
Blue-collar	474	38	34	184	34	32	8.6	8.4
Other	232	13	27	37	32	33	8.5	8.4
Different 3-digit, 1966 and 1976								
White-collar in 1976	389	22	23	84	23	27	5.9	6.9
Blue-collar in 1976	591	42	36	258	33	32	8.7	8.4
Other in 1976	170	36	24	65	30	32	7.8	8.1

Table A-4 (continued)

Characteristic	Percent with some unemployment			Persons with some unemployment					
					Cumulative number of weeks		Unemployment ratio[c]		
	n	Unadjusted	Adjusted	n	Unadjusted	Adjusted	Unadjusted	Adjusted	
Class of worker/industry			**			**		**	
Self-employed, 1966 and 1976									
1976	313	10	22	32	34	37	9.4	9.8	
Government, 1966 and 1976	255	9	18	24	20	23	6.0	6.7	
Private wage and salary, 1966 and 1976									
Construction in 1966	123	81	62	95	56	54	14.3	13.7	
Manufacturing in 1966	573	34	36	202	25	27	6.2	7.0	
Service in 1966	450	27	28	125	24	26	5.9	6.6	
Other in 1966	90	42	33	38	36	38	9.6	9.8	
Other, 1966 and 1976	436	34	23	165	30	25	7.7	6.4	
Tenure in current or last job, 1966			**						
Less than 1 year	214	55	41	120	36	31	9.2	8.0	
1-4 years	363	37	31	143	32	33	8.2	8.4	
5-9 years	321	25	26	86	31	32	7.7	8.0	
10-19 years	642	26	29	173	24	29	6.1	7.3	
20 or more years	670	19	24	137	29	30	7.5	7.7	
Retirement and mobility status			**			**		**	
Retired	414	37	36	162	34	37	9.3	9.7	
Never retired									
Same employer, 1966-1976	1101	12	16	146	16	18	4.0	4.5	
Changed employer, 1966-1976	713	48	44	361	32	30	8.0	7.6	

						**		**
Commitment to work, 1966[a]			+					
High	1777	27	28	512	30	30	7.7	7.8
Low	457	34	32	166	33	35	8.5	8.8
Locus of control (Rotter I-E Scale, 1969)			*					
Internal	815	24	26	204	27	28	6.7	7.2
External	1010	32	30	343	32	31	8.4	8.1
Number of years of less than continuous labor force participation[b]			**			+		
None	757	22	26	169	34	36	8.2	8.7
1	766	27	27	226	28	29	6.8	7.2
2-3	629	37	32	242	32	30	8.5	8.0
4-7	96	50	44	50	27	24	8.8	7.8
R^2 (adjusted)			.25			.21		.20

a. See text footnote 11.

b. I.e., less than 52 weeks.

c. (Weeks unemployed/weeks in labor force) x 100.

**F-ratio is significant at $\alpha = .01$.

*F-ratio is significant at $\alpha = .05$.

+F-ratio is significant at $\alpha = .10$.

Table A-5
Incidence and Duration of Unemployment, 1968-1978, by Selected Characteristics: Women 26-34 in 1978 (MCA Results)

Characteristic	Percent with some unemployment			Persons with some unemployment					
					Cumulative number of weeks			Unemployment ratio[d]	
	n	Unadjusted	Adjusted	n	Unadjusted	Adjusted		Unadjusted	Adjusted
Total sample	3031	68	68 **	2148	20	20 **		12.0	12.0 **
Race			**			**			**
Whites	2211	66	66	1465	18	18		10.8	11.4
Blacks	820	83	79	683	31	28		18.5	15.1
Age (1978)			**			**			**
26-29	1533	76	71	1208	20	19		11.2	11.1
30-34	1498	60	65	940	19	21		12.9	13.0
Marital and family status									
Married 1968 and 1978			+			**			*
Child(ren) < 6, 1968 and 1978	185	64	68	121	16	17		19.2	13.0
Child(ren) < 6, 1968 or 1978	547	57	64	322	17	19		13.9	11.6
No child(ren) < 6 either year	115	61	69	70	21	23		10.0	12.4
Married 1968, not married 1978									
Child(ren) < 6, 1968 and/or 1978	157	78	74	127	23	20		18.3	14.0
No child(ren) < 6 either year	48	66	72	33	16	17		5.8	11.6

Not married 1968 and 1978								
No child(ren) < 6								
either year	458	73	71	346	25	24	10.6	13.4
Others	243	82	73	204	31	27	19.4	14.5
Not married 1968, married 1978								
Child(ren) 1978	784	70	67	566	17	17	9.9	10.9
No child(ren) 1978	470	70	68	341	18	18	8.8	10.9
Health			**					*
No limitations	2484	66	67	1718	19	19	10.8	11.5
Limitations in 1968 and/or 1978	540	76	74	424	22	21	16.3	13.1
Training			+					+
None	1002	68	67	706	20	19	15.3	11.9
Prior to 1968, none later	178	53	62	97	16	17	11.2	12.7
Prior to 1968 and later	467	64	71	307	17	18	9.8	10.4
None prior to 1968, some later	1373	72	68	1034	21	21	10.7	12.5
Local unemployment rate, 1968			**					
Nonmigrants								
3.8 percent or lower	88	45	58	42	24	22	15.0	13.4
Over 3.8 percent	110	70	76	78	21	19	14.3	10.4
Migrants	2833	69	68	2028	20	20	11.8	12.0

Table A-5 (continued)

| Characteristic | Percent with some unemployment | | | Persons with some unemployment | | | | | |
| | | | | | Cumulative number of weeks | | Unemployment ratio[d] | |
	n	Unadjusted	Adjusted	n	Unadjusted	Adjusted	Unadjusted	Adjusted
Years of schooling, 1978			**			**		**
Same in 1968 and 1978								
Less than 12	515	75	70	399	23	21	20.4	13.8
12	882	58	63	535	17	18	10.7	11.5
13-15	180	55	61	105	14	15	8.5	10.3
16 or more	84	43	56	37	13	14	9.7	11.7
Different in 1968 and 1978								
Less than 12	104	87	78	90	34	32	23.8	17.1
12	402	80	72	333	23	21	12.1	12.4
13-15	353	76	72	272	18	19	8.0	11.2
16 or more	507	74	72	375	19	20	8.5	11.0
Occupation			**			**		**
Same 1-digit, 1968 and 1978								
White-collar	654	54	65	366	14	16	9.3	11.4
Blue-collar	122	65	73	85	23	21	14.5	11.7
Other	194	62	63	132	19	18	18.8	13.6
Different 1-digit, 1968 and 1978								
White-collar in 1978	938	72	69	685	17	18	8.4	10.1
Blue-collar in 1978	268	81	77	225	26	25	14.6	13.3
Other in 1978	288	70	69	212	23	21	14.5	12.7

Class of worker/industry			**			**		
Government, 1968 and 1978	203	48	61	109	17	20	9.6	11.4
Private wage and salary, 1968 and 1978								
Agriculture in 1968	72	82	67	62	21	13	16.8	8.2
Manufacturing in 1968	328	65	72	222	20	22	11.9	12.9
Transportation and utilities in 1968	77	58	72	44	19	24	11.0	14.7
Trade in 1968	403	75	73	303	17	19	10.9	12.2
Finance in 1968	91	47	63	46	18	23	8.7	12.2
Service in 1968	540	73	71	410	20	20	12.8	12.6
Other in 1968	6	a	a	4	a	a	a	a
Other, 1968 and 1978	750	66	65	495	19	21	9.1	12.2
Tenure in current or last job, 1968			**			**		*
Less than 1 year	1401	70	67	1009	18	19	10.2	11.4
1-2 years	523	59	64	323	18	19	10.6	11.2
3 or more years	303	53	58	169	18	18	10.1	11.8
Mobility status			**					**
Same employer, 1968-1978	753	52	55	416	19	19	14.1	12.8
Changed employer, 1968-1978	2073	74	73	1579	20	20	8.2	8.9
Commitment to work, 1970[b]			*			**		**
High	904	65	69	624	22	22	9.0	11.8
Low	576	67	72	393	18	19	9.2	10.2
Locus of control (Rotter I-E Scale, 1970)								
Internal	1086	66	67	752	19	19	11.1	11.8
External	1665	69	69	1200	20	20	12.3	12.1

Table A-5 (continued)

Characteristic	Percent with some unemployment			Persons with some unemployment					
					Cumulative number of weeks		Unemployment ratio[d]		
	n	Unadjusted	Adjusted	n	Unadjusted	Adjusted	Unadjusted	Adjusted	
Number of years of less than continuous labor force participation[c]			**					**	
None	71	24	34	18	15	15	a	a	
1	150	54	59	83	20	20	4.7	7.9	
2-3	505	62	59	325	19	18	5.7	8.4	
4-5	850	75	70	658	21	20	7.8	10.5	
6-7	1455	70	72	1064	19	20	17.2	14.4	
R^2 (adjusted)			.15			.09		.42	

a. Percentage not shown when base is fewer than 25 sample cases.

b. See text footnote 11.

c. I.e., less than 52 weeks.

d. (Weeks unemployed/weeks in labor force) x 100.

**F-ratio is significant at $\alpha = .01$.

*F-ratio is significant at $\alpha = .05$.

+ F-ratio is significant at $\alpha = .10$.

Table A-6
Incidence and Duration of Unemployment, 1967-1977, by Selected Characteristics: Women 40-54 in 1977 (MCA Results)

Characteristic	Percent with some unemployment			Persons with some unemployment					
					Cumulative number of weeks		Unemployment ratio[d]		
	n	Unadjusted	Adjusted	n	Unadjusted	Adjusted	Unadjusted	Adjusted	
Total sample	3343	40	40 **	1401	24	24 **	15.6	15.6 **	
Race			**			+		+	
Whites	2377	39	39	922	28	27	15.3	15.3	
Blacks	966	48	46	479	23	23	17.2	17.3	
Age (1977)			**			*		+	
40-44	1104	45	44	521	21	23	14.2	14.2	
45-49	1082	39	39	445	24	24	17.1	17.1	
50-54	1157	36	37	435	26	24	15.7	14.5	
Marital and family status Married 1967 and 1977			**			*			
Child(ren) < 16, 1967 and 1977	866	40	38	359	20	21	18.8	15.0	
Child(ren) < 16, 1967 or 1977	1065	35	36	381	24	24	14.6	15.2	
No child(ren) < 16 either year	326	37	41	127	32	32	17.0	18.1	

Table A-6 (continued)

Characteristic	Percent with some unemployment			Persons with some unemployment					
					Cumulative number of weeks		Unemployment ratio[d]		
	n	Unadjusted	Adjusted	n	Unadjusted	Adjusted	Unadjusted	Adjusted	
Married 1967, not married 1977									
Child(ren) < 16, 1967 and/or 1977	336	54	50	184	22	21	12.4	14.7	
No child(ren) < 16 either year	68	50	50	36	21	20	9.4	15.2	
Not married 1967 and 1977									
No child(ren) < 16 either year	211	34	43	77	24	23	11.6	16.8	
Others	295	51	46	154	29	27	18.3	17.1	
Not married 1967, married 1977	153	41	37	71	25	24	10.5	15.9	
Health								*	
No limitations	2181	38	40	866	23	24	14.5	15.8	
Limitations in 1967 and/or 1977	1099	43	39	510	25	24	17.9	15.8	
Training						**		**	
None	1361	42	39	608	26	24	19.1	17.4	
Prior to 1967, none later	571	38	39	227	25	26	17.0	16.1	
Prior to 1967 and later	790	37	41	305	22	25	12.8	14.6	
None prior to 1967, some later	621	41	40	261	19	19	10.6	12.8	

						+		
Local unemployment rate, 1967								
Nonmigrants		**		**				
3.8 percent or lower	1206	34	36	429	26	24	15.0	14.7
Over 3.8 percent	1451	38	39	604	25	25	18.0	16.5
Migrants	686	52	47	368	20	21	13.4	15.5
Years of schooling, 1967		**	**			**		*
Less than 12	1374	49	44	711	27	25	17.1	15.6
12	1403	36	38	506	22	24	14.7	16.0
13-15	285	40	42	115	16	18	11.5	12.5
16 or more	277	25	33	68	18	22	18.6	17.7
Occupation		**	**			**		*
Same 3-digit, 1967 and 1977								
White-collar	577	28	37	154	16	18	22.6	17.0
Blue-collar	194	56	54	110	28	22	18.6	16.5
Other	341	38	38	148	20	19	24.5	16.7
Different 3-digit, 1967 and 1977								
White-collar in 1977	1114	37	38	418	21	23	10.6	14.3
Blue-collar in 1977	350	61	54	220	33	31	13.5	14.9
Other in 1977	641	44	37	297	25	24	16.6	15.6

Table A-6 (continued)

Characteristic	Percent with some unemployment			Persons with some unemployment				
					Cumulative number of weeks		Unemployment ratio[d]	
	n	Unadjusted	Adjusted	n	Unadjusted	Adjusted	Unadjusted	Adjusted
Class of worker/industry			**			**		
Government, 1967 and 1977	354	22	35	76	23	28	16.6	13.9
Private wage and salary, 1967 and 1977								
Agriculture in 1967	55	42	32	29	32	29	33.2	20.8
Manufacturing in 1967	561	51	48	298	30	27	16.3	17.1
Transportation and utilities in 1967	95	37	45	33	25	30	15.6	17.2
Trade in 1967	492	47	44	241	22	21	16.4	15.2
Finance in 1967	115	22	27	26	12	15	15.7	13.7
Service in 1967	656	44	40	302	21	20	16.4	15.7
Other in 1967	14	a	a	5	a	a	a	a
Other, 1967 and 1977	855	37	35	331	21	23	12.3	14.8
Tenure in current or last job, 1967			*			**		*
Less than 1 year	742	48	42	374	27	28	20.2	17.5
1-4 years	1456	42	41	645	23	23	14.9	15.7
5-9 years	507	34	39	178	20	18	12.2	13.6
10 or more years	485	27	35	139	27	24	11.4	15.0
Mobility status			**			+		**
Same employer, 1967-1977	1303	24	27	338	21	21	12.7	11.4
Changed employer, 1967-1977	1678	51	50	890	24	24	9.1	10.9

	N	%	%	N	%	%	%	%
Commitment to work, 1967[b]		**					**	
High	1229	36	37	466	24	22	9.0	12.8
Low	758	38	36	305	25	22	10.7	14.4
Locus of control (Rotter I-E Scale, 1969)							+	
Internal	1071	37	38	415	21	22	13.7	14.1
External	1823	41	40	782	25	24	16.5	16.4
Number of years of less than continuous labor force participation[c]		**				**	**	
None	249	17	24	46	26	28	6.2	11.5
1	402	26	31	118	24	22	6.2	10.4
2-3	918	42	41	402	27	27	8.5	12.6
4-5	985	49	46	502	25	25	14.0	15.0
6-7	789	40	39	333	16	16	31.2	22.6
R^2 (adjusted)		.16	.16			.10	.45	

a. Percentage not shown when base is fewer than 25 sample cases.

b. See text footnote 11.

c. I.e., less than 52 weeks.

d. (Weeks unemployed/weeks in labor force) x 100.

**F-ratio is significant at $\alpha = .01$.

*F-ratio is significant at $\alpha = .05$.

+ F-ratio is significant at $\alpha = .10$.

Table A-7
Average Hourly Earnings (Cents per Hour) in 1976, by Unemployment Experience 1966-1976: Multiple Regression Results for Two Male Cohorts

Variable	Men 26-34		Men 55-69	
	Coefficient	t	Coefficient	t
Moderate unemployment (1-65 weeks)[a]	-47	-2.92	-25	-1.47
Chronic unemployment (66 or more weeks)[a]	-143	-3.58	-73	-1.43
Average hourly earnings, 1966 (cents)	1.27	14.71	2.56	39.33
Moderate absence from labor force, 1966-1976[b]	22	1.28	-15	-0.96
Substantial absence from labor force, 1966-1976[b]	-13	-0.30	-50	-1.32
Black	-98	-4.14	-18	-0.72
Acquisition of training, 1966-1976	63	3.49	47	2.81
Health limitation 1966, not 1976	-13	-0.43	-19	-0.71
Health limitation 1976, not 1966	4	0.13	18	0.83
Health limitation 1966 and 1976	-63	-1.25	-37	-1.22
Migrant, same region[c]	1	0.07	-8	-0.35
Migrant, north to south[c]	-0.9	-0.02	-74	-1.18
Migrant, south to north[c]	139	3.79	142	1.94
Completed 1 additional year of school, 1966-1976[d]	9	0.41	d	d
Completed 2 additional years of school, 1966-1976[d]	23	0.90	d	d
Completed 3 additional years of school, 1966-1976[d]	-16	-0.42	d	d
Completed 4 or more additional years of school, 1966-1976[d]	-19	-0.42	d	d
N	920		1176	
R^2 (adjusted)	0.29		0.60	

a. Reference group consists of individuals with no unemployment during the decade.

b. For men 26-34, moderate absence is 1-60 weeks and substantial absence is 61 or more weeks; for men 55-69, moderate absence is 1-30 weeks. In each case reference group are those with no weeks out of the labor force.

c. Reference group consists of those who were in same local labor market area in 1966 and 1976. Regions are defined as south and non-south (north).

d. Variable used only for men 26-34. Reference group are those whose reported years of schooling was the same in 1968 and 1978.

Table A-8
Average Hourly Earnings (Cents per Hour) in 1978,[a] by Unemployment Experience 1968-1978[a]: Multiple Regression Results for Two Female Cohorts

Variable	Women 26-34 Coefficient	Women 26-34 t	Women 40-54 Coefficient	Women 40-54 t
Moderate unemployment (1-65 weeks)[b]	-43	-2.27	-40	-2.91
Chronic unemployment (66 or more weeks)[b]	-186	-2.54	-32	-0.74
Average hourly earnings, 1968 (cents)	0.7	6.25	1.54	20.46
Moderate absence from labor force (1-60 weeks), 1968-1978[c]	30	0.90	-9	-0.55
Substantial absence from labor force (61 or more weeks), 1968-1978[c]	-38	-1.07	-58	-2.74
Black	-38	-1.4	13	0.79
Acquisition of training, 1968-1978	45	2.03	40	2.98
Health limitation 1968, not 1978	-39	-0.84	-22	-0.80
Health limitation 1978, not 1968	3	0.07	-43	-2.19
Health limitation 1968 and 1978	-121	-1.79	-36	-1.21
Migrant, same region[d]	38	1.16	50	3.05
Migrant, north to south[d]	-14	-0.31	-85	-1.75
Migrant, south to north[d]	29	0.54	-73	-1.15
Completed 1 additional year of school, 1968-1978[e]	60	2.15	e	e
Completed 2 additional years of school, 1968-1978[e]	91	3.10	e	e
Completed 3 additional years of school, 1968-1978[e]	67	1.77	e	e
Completed 4 or more additional years of school, 1968-1978[e]	125	4.15	e	e
Married, spouse present in 1968, not married, 1978[f]	84	2.34	-43	-2.44
Married, spouse present in 1978, not married, 1968[f]	8	0.43	-48	-1.82
Child(ren) in 1968, none in 1978[g]	-39	-1.50	7	0.62
Child(ren) in 1978, none in 1968[g]	-10	-0.47	84	1.79
n	698		1092	
R² (adjusted)	0.13		0.37	

a. The time period for women 40-54 is 1967-1977, and the dependent variable is average hourly earnings in 1977.
b. Reference group consists of individuals with no unemployment during the decade.
c. Reference group consists of individuals with no weeks out of the labor force.
d. Reference group consists of those who were in same local labor market area during the entire decade. Regions are defined as south and non-south (north).
e. Variable used only for women 26-34. Reference group are those whose reported years of schooling was the same in 1968 and 1978.
f. Reference group consists of women who were married in both years or not married in both years.
g. For women 26-34, children refers to those under 6; for women 40-54 children refers to those under 16. In each case, reference group is women who had children of these ages either in both years or in neither year.

Table A-9
Case Studies of Chronic Unemployment, 1966-1976: Men 26-34

Case no.	Age 1976	Race	Marital status 1966	Marital status 1976	Years of schooling 1966	Years of schooling 1976	Health[a]	Employment status, 1966[b]	Occupation[c] 1966	Industry[c] 1966	No. of years in 1966 job	Weeks out of labor force	Weeks unemployed	Employment status, 1976[b]	Occupation[c] 1976	Industry[c] 1976	No. of employers[d]	No. of occupations[e]
1	30	W	M	M	9	9	3	E	carpenter	construction	2	9	81	E	laborer	construction	5	2
2	34	W	M	M	11	11	0	E	road machine operator	construction	2	0	147	E	road machine operator	construction	2	1
3	30	W	M	M	8	8	0	E	laborer	primary metal mfg.	2	0	71	E	operative	chemical mfg.	5	6
4	30	B	M	M	12	13	0	E	operative	printing	1	9	75	E	office manager	(printing thru 1975)	2	4
5	33	W	M	M	11	11	0	E	fountain worker	retail trade	1	0	98	E	truck driver	transportation	6	3
6	28	B	U	U	6	7	0	E	farm laborer	agriculture	3	123	78	E	laborer	construction	8	4

7	29	W	U	U	6	6	0	E	garage laborer	repair service	1	128	94	E	janitor	transportation	3	4
8	34	W	M	M	8	8	0	E	auto mechanic	repair service	1	26	82	U	auto mechanic	retail trade	4	2
9	28	W	M	D	9	12	3	E	assembler	non-durable mfg.	2	47	148	E	taxi-driver	transportation	3	3
10	30	W	U	U	10	10	2	E	operative	lumber mfg.	1	26	72	E	laborer	personal service	6	7

For footnotes, see table A-12.

Table A-10
Case Studies of Chronic Unemployment, 1966-1976: Men 55-69

Case no.	Age 1976	Race	Marital status 1966	Marital status 1976	Years of schooling 1966	Years of schooling 1976	Health[a]	Employment status, 1966[b]	Occupation[c] 1966	Industry[c] 1966	No. of years in 1966 job	Weeks out of labor force	Weeks unemployed	Employment status, 1976[b]	Occupation[c] 1976	Industry[c] 1976	No. of employers[d]	No. of occupations[e]
11	60	B	S	D		11	0	E	decorator	business service	3	0	66	E	gardener	business service	6	6
12	56	W	M	M		11	0	E	manager	metal mfg.	9	0	66	U	manager	metal mfg.	1	1
13	62	W	M	M		8	3	E	loom fixer	textile mfg.	20	6	72	U	loom fixer	textile mfg.	1	1
14	60	W	M	M		7	0	E	craftsman	construction	NA	0	178	E	craftsman	construction	5	1
15	58	W	M	M		10	0	E	carpenter	construction	26	10	111	E	carpenter	construction	4	1
16	55	W	M	M		8	1	U	truck driver	construction	NA	11	108	E	foreman	mining	2	3
17	62	W	M	M		10	3	U	operative	apparel mfg.	NA	27	84	OLF	operative	apparel mfg.	2	1

18	57	W	W	D	9	0	E	mill-wright	food mfg.	20	68	66	E	guard	business service	6	3
19	63	W	M	D	12	2	U	cook	restaurant	4	47	77	U	cook	restaurant	3	1
20	56	B	M	M	8	3	E	truck driver	transport	0	87	105	E	self-employed laborer	NA	3	6

For footnotes, see table A-12.

Table A-11
Case Studies of Chronic Unemployment, 1968-1978: Women 26-34

Case no.	Age 1976	Race	Marital status 1968	Marital status 1978	Age of youngest child 1968	Age of youngest child 1978	Years of schooling 1968	Years of schooling 1978	Health[a]	Employment status, 1968[b]	Occupation[c] 1968	Industry[c] 1968	Weeks out of labor force	Weeks unemployed	Employment status, 1978[b]	Occupation[c] 1978	Industry[c] 1978	No. of employers[d]	No. of occupations[e]
21	28	W	U	U	none	none	12	12	0	U	inspector	metal mfg.	1	128	E	clerical worker	bakery products	3	4
22	30	W	U	U	none	none	12	12	0	U	NA	retail trade	4	98	E	typist	federal public admin.	3	5
23	32	W	U	M	none	1	16	17	1	E	professional technical	advertising	35	67	E	self-employed	retail trade	5	6
24	27	B	S	S	under 1	7	10	13	0	E	operative	textile mfg.	42	69	E	messenger	business services	4	7
25	29	B	U	U	none	9	12	12	0	U	typist	local public admin.	7	72	E	inspector	machine mfg.	5	4
26	27	W	M	M	none	4	10	10	2	OLF	babysitter	private household	240	88	U	cook	restaurant	3	4

27	30	W	U	M	none	4	14	17	2	OLF	clerical worker	business services	146	100	OLF	professional technical	wholesale trade	2	3
28	31	W	M	M	none	7	12	12	0	E	medical technician	hospital	22	73	OLF	medical technician	hospital	2	1
29	34	W	M	D	1	5	10	0	OLF	waitress	restaurant	294	75	U	sewer, mfg.	apparel mfg.	1	3
30	27	B	U	M	none	7	11	12	0	U	clerical worker	education-al services	284	95	OLF	sales worker	shoe store	0	2

For footnotes, see table A-12.

Table A-12
Case Studies of Chronic Unemployment, 1967-1977: Women 40-54

Case no.	Age 1977	Race	Marital status 1967	Marital status 1977	Age of youngest child, 1967	Child(ren) under 16, 1977	Years of schooling	Health[a]	Employment status, 1967[b]	Occupation[c] 1967	Industry[c] 1967	Weeks out of labor force	Weeks unemployed	Employment status, 1977	Occupation 1977	Industry 1977	No. of employers[d]	No. of occupations[e]
31	43	W	W	W	NA	No	10	0	OLF	waitress	restaurant	26	72	E	telephone operator	business services	3	3
32	47	W	M	M	10	No	10	3	U	operative	warehousing and storage	11	77	E	sales-worker	drug stores	1	2
33	53	W	M	M	9	No	12	0	E	operative	canning mfg.	0	158	E	operative	canning mfg.	1	1
34	54	W	M	M	13	No	12	0	E	self-employed office manager	retail trade	0	85	E	self-employed office manager	retail trade	4	5
35	40	B	M	M	8	No	12	0	E	assembler	machinery mfg.	0	98	E	hospital attendant	hospital	3	3
36	48	W	M	M	9	No	6	2	OLF	private household worker	private household service	100	145	E	cook	lodging services	2	4

37	51	W	M	M	10	No	12	0	E	operative	canning mfg.	203	123	OLF	operative	canning mfg.	1	2
38	54	B	S	W	11	No	10	0	U	sewer, mfg.	apparel mfg.	129	138	E	clerical	education-al services	1	2
39	53	W	M	M	9	No	12	0	E	steward	entertain-ment services	147	92	U	clerical worker	retail trade	3	4
40	50	W	M	M	8	No	7	0	OLF	sewer, mfg.	apparel mfg.	269	80	OLF	sewer, mfg.	apparel mfg.	1	2

a. Health is coded as follows:

0 - No health limitations, 1966 and 1976

1 - Health limited in 1966 and 1976

2 - Health limited in 1966, not in 1976

3 - Health limited in 1976, not in 1966

b. Employment status as of the calendar week preceding the survey.

c. Occupation (3-digit) and industry (2-digit) of job held in week preceding survey, if employed at that time; otherwise, the occupation and industry of most recent job.

d. Number of employers is a minimum estimate, since it simply counts the number of different employers reported for the week preceding each survey (self-employment is considered to be an employer). An employer for whom a respondent worked at sometime other than the week preceding the survey would not be included.

e. Number of different three-digit occupations reported by respondent for job held in week preceding each survey or (if not employed at that time) in most recent job.

References

Andrisani, Paul and Nestel, Gilbert. "Internal-External Control and Labor Market Experience." In Parnes, Herbert S. et al., *The Pre-Retirement Years,* Vol. 4. U.S. Department of Labor Manpower R & D Monograph No. 15. Washington: U.S. Government Printing Office, 1975.

Center for Human Resource Research. *National Longitudinal Handbook.* Columbus: The Ohio State University, 1982.

Clark, Kim B. and Summers, Lawrence H. "Labor Market Dynamics and Unemployment: A Reconsideration." *Brookings Papers on Economic Activity,* 1: 1979, pp. 13-72.

Corcoran, Mary and Hill, Martha S. "The Incidence and Consequences of Short- and Long-Run Unemployment." Chapter 1 in Duncan, Greg J. and Morgan, James N. (eds.) *Five Thousand American Families: Patterns of Economic Progress,* Vol. 7. Ann Arbor: Institute for Social Research, University of Michigan, 1979.

Dickinson, Jonathan. "Labor Supply of Family Member." Chapter 4 in Morgan, James N. et al., *Five Thousand American Families: Patterns of Economic Progress,* Vol. 1. Ann Arbor: Institute for Social Research, University of Michigan, 1974.

Feldstein, Martin S. "The Importance of Temporary Layoffs: An Empirical Analysis." *Brookings Papers on Economic Activity,* 3: 1975, pp. 724-745.

Fleisher, Belton M. and Kniesner, Thomas J. *Labor Economics: Theory, Evidence, and Policy,* 2nd Edition. Englewood Cliffs, NJ: Prentice Hall, Inc., 1980.

Gramlich, Edward M. "The Distributional Effects of Higher Unemployment." *Brookings Papers on Economic Activity,* 2: 1974, pp. 293-336.

Kohen, Andrew I. "Cumulative Duration and Spells of Unemployment Over a Two-Year Period: Out-of-School Youth." Chapter 3 in Kohen, Andrew I. and Parnes, Herbert S., *Career Thresholds: A Longitudinal Study of the Educational and Labor Market Experience of Male Youth.* U.S. Department of Labor Manpower R & D Monograph No. 16. Washington: U.S. Government Printing Office, 1971.

Lippman, Steven A. and McCall, John J. "The Economics of Job Search: A Survey." *Economic Inquiry,* 2: 1976.

Parnes, Herbert S. and Nestel, Gilbert. "The Incidence, Distribution, and Correlates of Unemployment Over a Decade, by Age and Race." *American Statistical Association 1980 Proceedings of the Social Statistics Section,* August 11-14, 1980, pp. 401-406.

Solow, Robert M. "On Theories of Unemployment." *American Economic Review,* 1: 1980.

U.S. Department of Labor, *Employment and Training Report of the President,* 1980.